Help for
the Lonely Child

Help for the Lonely Child

STRENGTHENING SOCIAL PERCEPTION

Ernest, Rita, and Paul Siegel

A SUNRISE BOOK | E. P. DUTTON | NEW YORK

Grateful acknowledgment is given Scholastic Magazines, Inc., for permission to reprint material from *Smiles, Nods and Pauses* by Dorothy Grant Hennings. Copyright © 1974 by Dorothy Grant Hennings.

Library of Congress Cataloging in Publication Data
Siegel, Ernest.　　Help for the lonely child.
Bibliography: p.　　Includes index.
1. Child psychology. 2. Nonverbal communication (Psychology).
3. Social perception. 4. Loneliness.
I. Siegel, Rita, joint author.　　II. Siegel, Paul, 1954–
joint author.　　III. Title.
HQ773.S35　1978　155.4　77–18746
ISBN: 0–87690–289–1
Published simultaneously in Canada by Clarke, Irwin & Company Limited, Toronto and Vancouver

10 9 8 7 6 5 4 3 2 1

First Edition

CONTENTS

Note: Since there is no nonsexist pronoun in English which refers to a person, the word "she" will be used to indicate a teacher at the primary and secondary school level. We do not mean to imply that only women teach school.

PREFACE

Students of communication are familiar with the story of Von Osten and his remarkable horse. Some years ago, in Germany, he began training his horse, soon dubbed "Clever Hans," to respond to arithmetic examples by tapping his front hoof a given number of times. Hans enlarged his repertoire to telling time, recalling musical pitch, and after his owner showed him how to translate the alphabet into a specific number of taps, answering a variety of questions on almost any subject. The questions could be spoken or in writing. The animal seemed to have a thorough understanding of the German language and to be unusually intelligent, even by human standards.

After performing successfully for years, the "secret" was finally unearthed. An experiment was set up whereby one person whispered a number in his right ear and another person whispered a second number in his left ear. Hans was to add the two together, but he was unable to produce the correct number of taps. Further investigation led to the discovery that the horse answered questions correctly only if an individual who knew the answer was in his line of vision. Evidently, even unbeknown to Von Osten, the horse's cue to start tapping was the observer's "body language" messages of expectancy (standing on edge, so to speak). When he reached the correct number of hoofbeats, other signals (body relaxation, slight movement of head, a visible sigh of relief, and so forth) would ensue and it was these visual prompts that cued Hans to stop tapping.

In retrospect, the entire phenomenon probably occurred randomly at first. Very likely the horse was rewarded for his display of "intelligence." This reinforced the chances for the recurrence of this behavior, that is, simply to start tapping anytime an "on edge" cue is perceived and to stop on the "relaxation" cue. It might even be that the onlookers' nervousness triggered nervous behavior in the animal (that is, tapping) and the human relaxation signals were translated into relaxed animal behavior (cessation of tapping).

The point is that nonverbal communication signals are transmitted and are read constantly in all social situations. Haven't most of us, when disinterested in any setting ranging from a classroom to an informal conversation with one or more acquaintances, mastered the art (and generally subconsciously, at that) of *looking like* we're paying attention; and, conversely, don't many teachers and speakers instinctively know when disinterest sets in? Don't we sense whether a person is "up" or "down," whether a speaker is serious or kidding around, when one is suspicious, hostile, sympathetic, impatient, bored, secretive, evasive, artificially polite, stern? Don't we constantly interpret the messages of raised eyelids, the shrugging of shoulders, wringing of hands, lowering of the voice, the stare, the upward gaze, the upright posture? As a rule, these signals are emitted unwittingly and unintentionally, and we, in turn, read them effortlessly and almost naturally. Or so it seems.

But what if an individual (whether because of neurological handicap, emotional disturbance, or some specific learning disability) has difficulty in interpreting these cues and in fact is quite inept in social perception across the board? He obviously will miss a great deal of the message. How much? Considerably more than most people would imagine. Surprisingly, it has been found that when a person talks, the words themselves account for less than ten percent of what he communicates. The major portion is conveyed by manner of speech, facial expression, and body language.

This is ironic when we consider the school curriculum with respect to the so-called language arts. With the exception of some of the readiness activities—for example, finger play songs, listening skills —encountered largely in kindergarten and the lower elementary grades, the major focus throughout the school years is upon reading, rounded out by penmanship, spelling, grammar, vocabulary, and creative writing. In short, we teach *words* with a vengeance. Interpreting facial expressions, "reading" body language, judging personal and social space, associating specific tones of voice with the speaker's intent—all of these remain totally uncharted syllabi.

True, most people learn these tangentially, but what of the others? Must their *current* deficits in nonverbal communication skills leave them *forever* on the periphery, individuals who remain isolated from the mainstream of social intercourse, friendless and utterly lonely? *Or can they learn via specific instruction what most of us learn incidentally?* Since many young people who are deficient in social perception possess normal to above normal intelligence and are highly motivated to improve, the answer would seem to be yes.

ACKNOWLEDGMENTS

From the very inception of this project, we began to gather information and ideas from various sources. The suggestions as well as the encouragement from friends and colleagues are deeply appreciated. For having critically reviewed portions of the manuscript and for serving as much-needed "sounding boards," we are grateful to Professors Marvin Cohn, Roberta Wiener, Joan Bildman, Edith Billig, Judith Chusid, Jay Smith, and Ruth Gold, all of Adelphi University's Education Department; Amy Stoller of the Drama Department at Mills College, Oakland, California; graduate student Manny Berger, Public Health Department, Harvard University; and to Dolores Richardson and staff at the Rose Street Community Child Care Center in Berkeley.

Various state and regional Association for Children with Learning Disabilities (A.C.L.D.) chapters invited us to address their annual conferences concerning the problems of lonely and socially imperceptive children. Among these were the Quebec, Ohio, New York, Massachusetts, and Missouri chapters. University Special Education departments conducted similar programs and were kind enough to invite our participation: University of Arkansas Medical

Center, Little Rock; University of Missouri, Columbia; McMasters University, Toronto.

Sister Teresita McCardle of the College of New Rochelle was extremely gracious and supportive in making its Special Education Materials Resource Center available to us for research.

Finally, we are especially thankful to the many students in our college courses for their opinions, suggestions, and interest.

Ernest Siegel
Rita Siegel
Paul Siegel

PART 1

Introduction and Background

The individual who is ineffective in nonverbal communication often makes poor social judgments, does not readily grasp others' intentions, moods, and reactions (and hence, does not modify his behavior accordingly), and, in general, comes across as "different." His "differentness" causes him to be rejected by his peers, and this in turn lowers his self-esteem. He gradually stops trying to gain social acceptance and ultimately settles for chronic loneliness.

Conversely, the individual who is lonely for whatever reason misses out on the "education" provided by those social experiences in which his nonhandicapped counterpart participates so naturally. He is denied those countless training and practice sessions, most of which occur outside of the classroom, that involve receiving and expressing myriad nonverbal communication signals and the simultaneous "give-and-take" of conversation.

Thus, poor social perception can very likely cause loneliness, but it can also be seen as an effect of it.

CHAPTER 1
Loneliness

This is a book for parents and educators of children who are lonely. We hope to aid these parents and teachers in identifying those factors that produce and sustain loneliness, and in acquiring skills that will help them help the lonely child.

Before proceeding any further, two important qualifying statements should be made:

1. *We are all lonely from time to time.* Who among us has not felt rejected, unwanted, unloved, perhaps even unworthy of love? Haven't we all sometimes felt that genuine understanding between ourselves and another person was an unattainable goal? Further, we have all behaved inappropriately and gracelessly in numerous social settings. It is likely that we also share the experience of having indulged in self-deprecation stemming from our more awkward moments. Most of us have probably even contemplated suicide at some time.

Is everyone, then, "the lonely child"? Yes, and no. Yes, we all experience lonely feelings and exhibit inappropriate behavior. But the distinctive quality of the lonely child is that he does so more frequently and more pervasively.

When we feel "down," we can reasonably expect to feel more

cheery again in the near future. The lonely child's moroseness may not evaporate quite so predictably.

We are often able to realistically ascribe our depressions to particular events. We feel unloved *because* someone rejected us, we feel incompetent *because* we acted foolishly in a recent encounter. And we remind ourselves that neither we nor the world are perfect, that such things do occur, and that we will be able to work through our unpleasant feelings.

The lonely child usually cannot pinpoint the source of his discomfort. His loneliness is not bound to a specific incident, but to a whole history of failure in dealing with people. The lonely child is faced with such a high proportion of negative social experiences that to single out the especially painful one to blame his plight upon would be a waste of time. If asked, "What's wrong?" such a child might respond, "Everything."

When most of us feel lonely, we are able to appreciate the simple wisdom to be found in the maxim "count your blessings." When we do count our blessings, we usually conclude that we are indeed worthy of love and acceptance, that the vast majority of our interpersonal dealings brings us much joy. The lonely child is not so fortunate. He has a very small inventory of past successes upon which to draw. Moreover, his low image of himself can be such a prevailing theme that he fails to recognize whatever strengths he does possess. Attempting to console such a child with the suggestion that "things aren't so bad" is a dangerous tack, doomed to boomerang in at least two directions. First, he will know we are not really in tune with the depth of his emotions, that we do not understand his feelings. More importantly, we are invalidating those feelings completely, in effect saying that he is so imperceptive that he doesn't even know when to feel morose and when not to.

Although we all experience loneliness, the lonely child's experience of it is special, and it requires special handling.

2. *Loneliness is not an entirely negative experience.* "People who need people are the luckiest people in the world." This lyric to one of the best-selling songs of the 1960s seems to be a recipe for self-actualization. If we need people, and if we express that need successfully, then everything else will fall into place.

But shouldn't we sometimes need only ourselves? When we come across people who appear so gregarious that they are never alone, we often feel admiration, but we may also feel a bit of pity. We may imagine that such people cannot survive without the constant companionship they arrange for themselves.

Our negative reaction to excessive—almost compulsive—extroversion is probably related to our belief that being alone is often a good thing. We believe this to be true for ourselves, as well as for others, however socially facile they may appear.

Being alone enables us to slow down a bit, to discard our social faces, and to take account of ourselves. We can use our time alone to engage in activities that simply are not well-suited to a social setting—like reading and writing. Then there are activities that are frequently seen as social occasions, but that we may choose to do alone from time to time. Many of us enjoy attending a play or a concert alone. Doing so enables us to feel the event "sink in," unburdened by obligations to discuss our reactions immediately with a companion (1961, 102).

Clark Moustakas claims that loneliness is one of the few significant experiences left to modern man. It is through loneliness that he "discovers life, who he is, the meaning of his existence, and the true nature of his relations with others."

Why, then, don't we simply train the lonely child to use his time more constructively? If he learns to be at home with himself, and if he keeps fairly busy, he won't have time to feel lonely.

In fact, we do strongly advocate providing the lonely child with skills necessary for enjoying his time alone. However, we must recognize that this child's isolation is not chosen by him. His aloneness is not a quest for personal growth, but is the simple result of rejection by others.

For the lonely child, the accumulation of successful social encounters should be stressed. Only when his peers begin to accept him will he be able to experience aloneness on a volunteer basis. He will then be better able to skillfully exploit his time alone.

LONELINESS AND POOR
COMMUNICATION SKILLS

Danny is a young adult who complains of his great difficulty in meeting people. "No one I approach seems to listen. They don't care about what I have to say." Once, in a "rap" group Danny attends regularly, one of the other group members offered a possible explanation for Danny's poor luck in social situations.

"You know," Judy began, "I never met you before tonight. I knew very quickly, though, that I probably would not want to get to know you. 'Why?' I wonder now. I think it's because, when I heard you talking to the others in the waiting room earlier, your voice was so very loud. It really grates on me. It's not like a conscious decision I went through or anything, it's just that I felt like withdrawing, not wanting to deal with you."

Danny does not suffer from any measurable hearing loss. His inappropriately loud voice is a result of poor social perception. People who are socially imperceptive do indeed "grate" on us. Dealing with them can be a burden. In Danny's case, the problem is his voice modulation. Another socially imperceptive person may discomfort us by standing too close when she speaks. And another person may frustrate us by failing to perceive a most obvious "joking" tone of voice, thus restricting us to very literal and concrete statements.

Whatever the specific "symptom" of poor communication skill may be for a particular individual, the point is that social imperception can lead to rejection, and loneliness.

CONFORMITY IN COMMUNICATION

Listen to a group of three-year-olds talking. Young Sally may be telling her playmates about her new toy. "But you know what?" Ross interrupts. "My mommy is taking me to the circus tomorrow." "But guess what?" another child chimes in. "I saw this TV show last night, and there was this guy from outer space or something and he . . ."

These children are not having a true "conversation." Rather,

8

they are randomly verbalizing. Were it not for the perfunctory transitional statements ("But you know what?" and "But guess what?") we see no evidence that any one of them is accounting for the presence of the others.

As we grow older, we learn that successful communication requires that certain rules be followed. Conversations, we discover, generally entail two or more persons talking—about one thing at a time. We grow to accept the implications of the fact that our minds work immeasurably more quickly than our mouths. We are always thinking more than we are saying. We learn, too, that much of what we are thinking is extraneous and irrelevant. We are usually aware of our own breathing, the pressure of our clothing on our bodies, the temperature and noise level of the room. Such bits of consciousness are best filed and forgotten, unless they are the subject of the discussion at hand.

We learn that "But you know what?" and "Guess what?" are inadequate subject changers. They fail to acknowledge what the other person said. We devise more elaborate transitions ("Yeah, and that reminds me of the time when . . ."), and we try to decide if an attempt to steer the conversation in another direction is appropriate at all at any given moment.

This may sound a lot like conformity, and indeed it is. Conformity is not necessarily a dirty word. Without it, we would be unable to make even the most basic assumptions about others' behavior, since perceived similarities between past and present experiences would be useless. In short, chaos would result.

Most of the rules to which we conform in our everyday conversations are so basic that we do not think about them consciously. We fail to realize that we *learned* them somewhere along the way, and that others may not have learned them well enough.

The lonely child may need direct training in even the most basic rules. He will have to be told that people do not appreciate being interrupted when they are speaking. He will need practice in adjusting the volume of his voice so as to be heard, without speaking too loudly. This child will need well-planned remediation in precisely those social expectations that most of us honor so unthinkingly.

9

COMMUNICATION HELPS US
UNDERSTAND OURSELVES

We are forever seeking out others' subjective evaluations of us. Consider, for example, the overweight person who decides finally to shed his excess pounds. As he progresses in his diet and/or exercise regimen, he would like to feel he is succeeding. Certainly there are objective measures available to him. A reliable scale will prove to him that he is in fact losing weight. That his clothes fit more loosely and his belt needs to be taken in a few notches provide supporting evidence. But somehow, if he is like most dieters, he will find the struggle worthwhile only when he begins to hear from those around him that he *appears* thinner, and more attractive, to them.

Interpersonal communication is the prime source of information regarding how we are viewed by others. This information is essential in the formation of our self-concept. It is through communication with others that we *learn* what kind of person we are, what personality traits we are developing, where our specific strengths and weaknesses lie, how physically attractive we appear. We may even look to others to decide what kinds of emotions we are experiencing. In an experiment conducted by Stanley Schachter and Jerome Singer, subjects who were placed in the company of a happy person concluded that they too were happy, while those subjects who were paired with an angry person decided that they were also feeling angry.

Teachers of the lonely child should be especially sensitive to how his feelings and behavior can be shaped by those around him. Such a child is particularly likely to mirror the emotions of other people. If his classmates manifest some hostility, he will display even more. If his playmates begin to get a bit rowdy, he will reflect and *exaggerate* their rowdiness.

COMMUNICATION VS. DISCONFIRMATION

For most of us most of the time, interpersonal communication increases our understanding, bolsters our self-image, and makes us feel good. At least we work toward those ends. After all, we tend to exercise selectivity in choosing people with whom to interact. We tend to spend time with people we like and to avoid those we dislike. As such, we usually hear good things about ourselves.

This is not to suggest that we surround ourselves with sycophants. Indeed, one distinguishing quality of a friend is that he will risk telling us things we would rather not hear, in order to help us grow. Here too, though, we are being confirmed, if not flattered. Our value as a person is being respected and nurtured. Besides, most of us would rather have nasty things said about us than nothing at all. We would rather encounter disagreement, even hostility, than apathy. Our worst fear is to be ignored entirely.

Disconfirmation is the result of being met with complete apathy. It occurs when we are treated as if our opinions are of no consequence, as if we ourselves do not exist.

The lonely child is often confronted with disconfirming messages. Since he is a poor communicator, others may find interacting with him tedious and demanding. They may attempt to avoid him entirely. Rarely is he presented with either ego-satisfying "strokes" or with constructive criticism.

The lonely child can find himself in a vicious circle, with no visible escape. The harder he tries to fit in, the more painfully he is reminded that he simply does not fit in. He loses either way: "If he hears negative evaluation no matter how slight, he will likely feel anxiety; if he avoids evaluation he will derogate himself for being a coward" (Giffin and Patton, 1971, 27).

The overwhelming negative effects of continual disconfirmation cannot be emphasized enough. A "nonconscious ideology" may result whenever only one kind of message is received. We slowly lose the capacity to even *imagine* alternative conceptions of the world or of ourselves: "Only a very unparochial and intellectual fish is *aware* that his environment is wet. After all, what else could it be?" (Bem and Bem, 1970, 89).

Some sections of our society (for example, blacks, Native Americans, women, gays) have historically received a disproportionate number of "disconfirming" messages. When these people begin to form social movements to better their lot, a typical first step has been the creation of "consciousness-raising groups" for their own members. And this should not be at all surprising. After

11

all, the consciousness-raising group is specifically designed to provide members with the freedom and equipment necessary for "reprogramming" their own beliefs about themselves. It is in this setting that group members are encouraged to create for themselves the very same self-confirming messages (for example, "I am a worthwhile person." "I am 'OK.'") that have been denied them in the outside world (Clark, 1977, 50).

The lonely child may be victim of a "nonconscious ideology." He may not be able to even imagine himself being accepted by others, fitting in. He too is in need of reprogramming and needs to hear some ego-building messages.

Caution is advised here. The lonely child will recognize any lack of sincerity in our attempts to bolster his self-image. We cannot simply tell him he is charming and a joy to talk to if he knows otherwise.

One thing we can learn from the process of consciousness raising is that self-confirming messages, to be effective, have to begin from within.

The lonely child needs help in developing those social skills that will enable him to *correctly* see himself as attractive and likable. The direct strokes we wish to give to him will only be accepted after he has created meaningful strokes of his own.

ON THE IMPORTANCE OF NONVERBAL COMMUNICATION

A pupil says "There's nothing the matter" to his teacher, but in a shaky voice. He sounds as if he is holding back tears. A co-worker assures us that he is thoroughly enjoying our conversation, all the while glancing at his timepiece. Two lovers verbally remind each other of their devotion, but they tense and withdraw at the sign of any physical affection.

In each of these instances, the verbal and the nonverbal message conflict. We are swayed by the nonverbal. We seem to believe strongly in the adage "actions speak louder than words." Even when the "action" involved is simply listening, nonverbal cues dominate. If the "listener" is fidgeting, leaning away from us, or engaged in another activity, we don't feel attended to. And our

12

annoyance is not at all lessened should the listener be able to produce a verbatim account of what we said ("What do you mean, I'm not listening? I heard every word.") Communication is more than hearing words (Egan, 1975, 61).

The importance of nonverbal communication is not limited to those situations where verbal and nonverbal messages conflict. Adept use of nonverbal communication improves the quality of almost any speech or conversation. A "dynamic" speaker is recognized as such largely due to his use of gestures, eye contact, variation in pitch and volume, and not because of his choice of words alone.

In the next chapter we will discuss different kinds of nonverbal communication. We will see how the lonely child may be a poor interpreter and transmitter of many types of nonverbal messages.

REFERENCES

Bem, Daryl, and Bem, Sandra. "Case Study of a Non-Conscious Ideology: Training the Woman to Know Her Place." In Daryl Bem, *Beliefs Attitudes and Human Affairs*. Belmont, Calif.: Wadsworth 1970, pp. 89–99.

Clark, Don. *Loving Someone Gay*. Millbrae, Calif.: Celestial Arts, 1977.

Egan, Gerald. *The Skilled Helper: A Model for Systematic Helping and Interpersonal Relating*. Belmont, Calif.: Wadsworth, 1975.

Giffin, Kim, and Patton, Bobby. *Fundamentals of Interpersonal Communication*. New York: Harper & Row, 1971.

Moustakas, Clark E. *Loneliness*. Englewood Cliffs, N.J.: Prentice-Hall, 1961.

Rosenfeld, L. B. *Human Interaction in the Small Group Setting*. Columbus, Ohio: Charles E. Merrill, 1973.

Schachter, Stanley, and Singer, Jerome, "Cognitive, Social and Physiological Determinants of Emotional State." *Psychological Review* 69 (1962): 379–399.

CHAPTER 2
Nonverbal Communication

The title of this chapter suggests that there exists an entity, easily distinguishable from verbal communication, that can be accurately referred to as nonverbal. If verbal communication deals with the spoken word, then nonverbal communication must deal with all other media, such as facial expressions, posture, and body movement. But the line between verbal and nonverbal is fuzzy. The verbal message rarely occurs outside the nonverbal context. Both are communication events, the speech content itself and the vocal characteristics of the speaker. In reality, almost all communication is verbal *and* nonverbal. It would be more accurate to refer to verbal and nonverbal *components* of messages.

Nonverbal communication is inevitable whenever people come into contact with each other. Even the vacant staring into space in crowded subway cars communicates, perhaps saying "I will respect your privacy and I expect you to honor mine." *We cannot not communicate!* Awareness of this axiom should sensitize us to the fact that all of us—including the lonely child—are constantly sending unintentional messages and are interpreting others' "leaked" signals.

FUNCTIONS OF NONVERBAL MESSAGES

Nonverbal messages come in different forms and serve a number of different functions. Ekman and Friesen (1969) see four possible functions of nonverbal messages.

Frequently, nonverbal messages serve as "stand-ins" for verbal equivalents. Thus, we *wave* "hello" or "good-bye," we *motion* another "come," we *nod* "yes" and we *shake* our heads "no." Nonverbal messages are most likely to occur in this context when influences such as distance or noise level preclude successful vocal communication. The airline ground attendant *motions* the pilot and his plane into final resting position at the gate. The restaurant owner *signals* that a table for four is ready.

We learn to use nonverbal "stand-ins" by observation and imitation, rarely through direct training. Yet they can be quite complex, and the socially imperceptive may "flub" them. Consider the nonverbal convention established to advise a speaker he should talk louder. We cup our hand around our ear and look directly at the speaker. But look in a mirror as you perform this simple act. It looks silly and meaningless if you don't also assume a pained facial expression, almost implying that you are literally straining to hear. Without that pained expression, the "I can't hear you" message may not come through at all.

Another function of nonverbal messages is to "illustrate" an accompanying verbal message. If I relate to you how it felt to see an eagle fly, you might notice that my arms begin to rise in subdued imitation of flight. My hands might churn rhythmically as I describe the workings of a motor.

We do not typically plan our use of illustrating gestures. We expect them to occur naturally and unobtrusively. But the socially imperceptive may have difficulty, in at least two ways. First, the actual amount of their gesturing may be inappropriate. Too much movement appears frantic and can be highly distracting. Too little movement can bore us, leading us to believe that the speaker does not have his "heart" in his words. The second problem the socially imperceptive may face is one of timing. The child who tries to explain how angry his playmate made him will fail pathetically if

15

his fist-pounding gesture occurs a beat or two too late. Indeed, he may elicit laughter from his audience, which will re-create his anger anew.

Interestingly, political candidates, and actors—whose livelihoods depend upon the impression they make upon audiences—often include gesturing guides for themselves within the texts of their speeches. Similarly, the socially imperceptive may benefit from direct instruction in this area.

A third function of nonverbal communication is that it tells people how we are feeling. We do not usually need to tell our friends that we are sad. They can tell by observing our facial expression, monotonous speech pattern, and overall sluggishness.

The particular kinds and amount of feeling we choose to express nonverbally is only partly a function of the emotions we are actually experiencing. We do not simply "let loose" with all our feelings in most situations. Rather, we follow a tacitly prescribed set of "display rules" that determines what kinds of emotional display may be appropriate.

One such display rule is to de-intensify an emotion. We tend to downplay the joy we feel at defeating an opponent, for example. To do otherwise would be unsportsmanlike. Yet the socially inept child may in fact gloat at another's poor performance, showing total unawareness of his opponent's feelings.

In other settings, we might be required to overintensify a feeling. When we approach members of the bereaved family at a funeral, we may feel the need to appear even more remorseful and grief-stricken than we truly are. Less dramatically, we may exaggerate our joy at receiving a gift.

Sometimes the appropriate rule to follow is to appear completely affectless or neutral. A person who is very sad, but who does not wish others to fuss over him, may ward off attention by showing no emotion. An expert poker player can prevent his opponents from intuiting the value of his cards by appearing affectless. The socially imperceptive may fail to hold back inappropriate bursts of emotion, thereby opening themselves indiscriminately to strangers.

Nonverbal communication can also serve as a disguise, substituting one emotion for another. Perhaps you have had the experience of giving a party for a small group of friends. If an uninvited guest appears, might you not feel obliged to conceal your surprise and irritation with a show of pleased acceptance?

So far we have seen how nonverbal messages can "stand-in" for verbal ones, how they can "illustrate" conversations, and how they can reveal the feelings of the speaker. Still another function of nonverbal communication is to punctuate, or "regulate," the flow of conversation. Head nods (the nonverbal "mmm-hmm"), eyebrow raises, postural shifts, and varying eye contact may all serve in this capacity.

The interesting thing about nonverbal "regulators" is that we tend not to be aware of them unless they are removed. Try to pursue a casual conversation with a friend, all the while consciously avoiding the use of regulating acts. Very likely this will be an awkward encounter. Socially inept persons are probably not employing regulators successfully. Eye contact may be virtually non-existent and such positive reinforcers as nods and smiles are almost never used. These omissions do indeed make conversing with them awkward and uncomfortable. It is not surprising then that they are not the ones sought out as partners for small talk.

Regulators are very powerful conditioning tools. We like it when people nod as we talk, and we will unconsciously seek further nodding. In introductory psychology classes, instructors frequently play a game with students in order to convince even the most humanistically inclined that human behavior can be shaped and molded just as can those of laboratory animals.

The game consists of choosing a particular verbal behavior whose frequency we wish to increase. We might select the simple use of the first person singular pronoun, "I." A subject who is unaware of our intentions is engaged in conversation with the instructor, who skillfully adjusts his own use of regulators so as to reinforce the use of "I." The instructor leans forward with each occurrence, he nods attentively, his eye contact becomes more intense.

Invariably, the number of "I" 's increases during the course of the conversation. And the subject is typically unaware of the manipulation.

One especially mischievous college class, we hear, decided to get

17

back at the instructor. By carefully monitoring their use of regulators during lecture sessions, they were able to "push" the instructor into a tiny corner of the stage. He continued lecturing, fixed in that spot, for the duration of the hour.

NONVERBAL MEDIA

Nonverbal messages are sent through many different channels. These include body movement, use of space, grooming and clothing, eye contact, vocal quality, and facial expressions.

Body Movement

Ray Birdwhistell has made an extensive study of the ways people move their body while conversing. He has concluded that a nonverbal code of sorts exists in each society, similar in structure to language. In Birdwhistell's words, ". . . there are body behaviors which function like significant sounds, that combine into simple or relatively complex words, which are combined into much longer stretches of structured behavior like sentences or even paragraphs" (1970, 80). If we wanted to decide if someone is angry, for example, we should look not for one cue, but for a set of related behaviors. He may clench his fist, scratch himself, *and* rub under his nose with his finger (Knapp, 1972, 95).

Nonverbal codes are like spoken languages in another way. Our vocal cords are capable of producing innumerable different sounds. Only a small number of these, however, will be perceived as unique by the listener, and a smaller number still will be meaningful in a given language. Similarly, the human body is capable of extending and contorting into thousands of different shapes. The eyebrows, for example, can be kept in a relaxed position, or they can be raised or lowered in many small gradations. However, most of the gradations of movement are missed by the observer. Perhaps we can perceive only about five positions, from very raised to very lowered. Further, we may assign differing nonverbal meanings to even fewer positions. The raised positions, as a group, might signify inquisitiveness; the lowered positions could convey mild displeasure; and the relaxed position might be perceived as neutral in affect.

The most valuable lesson we can learn from Birdwhistell's research is that the link between nonverbal messages and perceived meaning is a highly complex one. The surface has just been scratched. Popular authors who suggest that particular sets of nonverbal behaviors necessarily *mean* "I am angry" or "I am attracted to you" do their readers a disservice. Just as "hello" can take on different meanings in different contexts, so can folded arms, crossed legs, and compressed nostrils.

Use of Space

Edward Hall is an anthropologist who believes that one important variable to consider when studying a social interaction is the amount of space the participants use to separate them. We all function as if we carried an imaginary bubble around us, enclosing a space that is perceived to be as much ours as is our own skin. The size of the bubble expands or contracts depending upon what kind of interaction we are experiencing. Hall sees four distinct levels of movable, or "informal" space. These are: (1) intimate distance, (2) personal distance, (3) social distance, and (4) public distance (1966, 116–125).

Intimate distance is experienced when our imaginary protective bubbles all but disappear. It is the distance used in lovemaking, wrestling, comforting, and protecting. We are so close to each other (usually touching, and certainly not more than eighteen inches apart) that our visual perception of each other is limited and distorted.

People often find intimate distance forced upon them—in subway cars, elevators, and other settings. An unstated system of rules governs us in such uncomfortable situations. In a packed elevator, passengers keep their hands at their sides and avoid eye contact with each other. Should actual body contact occur, muscles are tightened to convey that this unauthorized sensation is not enjoyable.

Imperceptive people usually do not function in accordance with the rather strict code required in these kinds of social encounters.

19

They may fail to step aside, stare too long or intently and, in general, interact poorly when in close proximity to strangers.

The next level of interpersonal spacing occurs when participants stand from one and a half to four feet apart. This level is aptly called *personal distance* and is reserved for conversations of a personal nature. Only people with whom we feel familiar and comfortable are allowed at this distance for a large parcel of time. Others may also enter, but usually only during greeting and leave-taking rituals.

More impersonal conversations are conducted at a distance of from four to twelve feet, which Hall calls *social distance*. People who work together tend to maintain a close social distance. Cocktail party conversations are typically conducted at this range.

As we approach the outer limits of social distance, we reach a point beyond which we can conveniently choose not to acknowledge another's presence. This is the point where *public distance* begins. At public distance (twelve feet and beyond), our conversations, if any, are of a relatively formal nature. We tend to choose our words carefully, trying more diligently to produce well-formed sentences than we might at closer range. Public speaking students are made keenly aware of the demands imposed by public distancing, as their friends and classmates suddenly become "the audience."

Generally, the use of space does not become a major issue in our interactions. It comes naturally, and we only think about it when a breakdown occurs. But when you and I *do fail* to establish a tacit agreement concerning the appropriate distance for our interaction, tension and misunderstanding result. We probably can all think of particular conversations during which we became aware of a nonverbal "jockeying for position," where the search for a comfortable conversational distance was anything but effortless. Perhaps furniture arrangement presented an obstacle. Should I raise my voice a bit or take the more aggressive course of moving my chair closer?

The parents or teacher of the lonely child should be sensitive to his use of space. Perhaps this child has a tendency to approach too closely, or not closely enough. In either event, he is likely to transmit messages he does not intend.

Grooming and Clothing

It is probably no great revelation that, if other factors remain constant, we tend to like physically attractive people more than we do unattractive people. This aesthetic preference seems to be formed at a young age. Dion and Berscheid (1971) studied interpersonal attraction patterns among nursery school students. Predictably, highly attractive students (as judged by independent raters) were most popular. This was especially true of the boys. Homely boys were seen as aggressive and even scary.

Our preference for dealing with pretty people seems to become even more pronounced in adolescence and young adulthood. Elaine Walster and her colleagues (1966, 508–516) found physical attractiveness the best single predictor of whether college freshman dance partners chose to date each other again. There is also evidence to suggest that our own self-image can temper our quest for attractive people. When we are not feeling very good about ourselves, we tend to prefer the company of people who are not quite so beautiful (Kiesler and Baral, n.d.).

To the extent that physical attractiveness is an inborn trait, the research pointing to its impact upon interpersonal relationships can only depress us. After all, we cannot change our genes. But a large part of our physical appeal is under our direct control. We *can* dress more attractively, we *can* maintain a well-groomed appearance, and we *can* assume a posture that communicates confidence. Indeed, much research indicates that people who do take pride in their appearance are viewed as more attractive and as more desirable.

Unfortunately, the lonely child has a very poor opinion of his own worth. This is frequently reflected in his disinterest in good grooming and in flattering clothing. The parent and teacher will, of course, attempt to improve his self-concept, but it is equally important to focus directly upon the symptoms of that poor self-image. Therefore, if guidance and sensitive assistance (not nagging) in achieving an attractive appearance are proffered, they may well result in a better appearance, a greater degree of acceptance, and, consequently, heightened self-esteem. Perhaps the lonely child can learn that if he feels good about himself, the good feelings will prove contagious.

21

Eye Contact

When people talk, they look at each other's eyes more frequently than at anything else, sometimes as much as seventy-five percent of the time (Harrison, 1974, 126). As such, eye contact should provide a wealth of information to the participants.

Eye contact is the best gauge we have when trying to see if the other fellow is listening. Indeed, the command to "pay attention" is primarily a request for more eye contact. When counselors are trained to listen to their clients' problems, one of the first lessons is in the use of eye contact. Insightful verbal responses are fine, but it is most essential that the client *feels* someone is listening (Brammer, 1973, 82).

Within a conversation, eye contact serves to punctuate the flow of conversation. It is most apparent when one speaker is finishing an utterance and is seeking a reply.

Another function of eye contact is that of initiating conversations. A skilled waiter has learned to maintain a delicate balance between appearing available for interaction without seeming pushy and hovering. His success, to a large degree, is owing to adept eye behavior.

Clearly, inept use of eye contact can result in awkward miscommunication. If we misread a perfunctory glance of acknowledgment as an open door to further communication, we may force an encounter on someone who does not seek it. Or we may interpret an upward glance as a sign that it is our turn to talk. If that gaze were really a signal that our partner was in need of "time out" to formulate his next statement, then our interruption will be most unwelcome.

Although eye contact is generally a good thing, it can be overdone. People do not like to be stared down, especially at close range. Teachers of children with perceptual impairments report that one child will frequently challenge another with "What are you staring at?"

The best way to develop skills in use of eye contact is simply to practice, and to consciously become aware of the cues presented. Students in communications classes are sometimes advised to "break the rules," to purposely maintain too little or too much eye contact and to note the results. In a supportive atmosphere, such experimentation can be helpful.

Vocal Quality

Whenever we talk to a person, we pay keen attention to his voice. Since the invention of the telephone, the voice has become, in many cases, the only clue available to us as we try to understand each other. How do we do it? Trager (1958, 1–12) suggests we listen for a number of different cues. We attend to *voice qualities,* like pitch range, rhythm control, resonance, and articulation. *Vocal characterizers,* including moaning, crying, yawning, and swallowing, are also perceived. We may note intentional *vocal qualifiers,* especially loudness and softness. *Vocal segregates,* such as "er," "uh," and "um" can tell us a great deal. Finally, we note how frequently and for how long there is no talking at all, how silences function in the conversation.

We can learn a great deal from just listening to the way people say things, even if we cannot understand the words. When we overhear the rumblings of a conversation in the next apartment, we know instantly whether the participants are having a fight or a party (Harrison, 1974, 111).

Skill in interpreting vocal cues can be of large importance because people do not always say what they mean. Frequently the true message is not in the words but in the speaker's voice. The clearest instances of this interaction occur when we purposely employ irony or sarcasm.

Sometimes our voices contradict our words in more subtle ways. Even if my words tell you that I am very interested in what you are saying, my voice may betray my true boredom. A "Hollywood invitation" ("Oh yes, we simply must get together for dinner sometime") is recognized as such largely on the basis of vocal cues. The socially imperceptive person may interpret this invitation literally, miss the *vacuous* politeness, and perhaps even press for more details ("When?").

Vocal messages are essential to effective communication even when they do not contradict the verbal content. I may tell you that I am angry with you. That alone is valuable information for you.

23

However, you should also note my tone of voice as I deliver my message. It is your best clue for deciding just how angry I am, and how wary you need be.

Facial Expressions

(Our facial expressions are probably the single most potent communicators of emotion.) A smile is all but synonymous with happiness, a frown with sadness. Even in the first few days of life, the human infant displays a longer fixation period for human faces than for designs or configurations (Fantz, 1963). And within several months, the infant learns to discriminate smiling faces from menacing ones, with only the former capable of eliciting a positive response (Spitz, 1946).

If we were to ask you to show us how you think you appear when you are angry, you would probably rely upon your facial muscles more than any others. This is true even though we would not have suggested that you concentrate on the *facial* expression of the emotion. You would have taken for granted that facial contortions and emotional displays go together.

We are often very aware of what kinds of messages our face portrays. Perhaps you have experienced the internal feedback of noting how quickly your own social smile disappeared when the person you were greeting passed out of view.

To the extent that we consciously manipulate our facial expressions, they communicate more of how we want to appear than of how we truly feel. We exert a great deal of energy in monitoring our own facial displays and adjusting them to fit different situations (Snyder, 1974). In our own society, for example, there seems to be a widely followed display rule governing the expression of sadness. Generally, we mask our sadness except from people to whom we feel close, and even then only in comfortable and supportive situations.

Many facial expressions, however, come through uncensored. Recent research techniques employing film or videotape have shown that our true feelings almost always are "leaked" at least for a fraction of a second (Haggard and Isaacs, 1966).

Perhaps the most important thing to remember about facial expressions is the notion, discussed earlier in this chapter, that we cannot *not* communicate. Our facial expressions may complement our verbal message, they may contradict it, or they may appear instead of it. Some message is always there. Even when we think we are deadpanning it, our faces are being read and interpreted.

How do we know that training in communication skills will help the lonely child?

So far we have discussed the different functions of nonverbal messages, and we have seen how these messages come from numerous sources. Throughout, we have stressed that the socially imperceptive may "miss the boat" and fail to absorb the truly important messages. The more socially inept a person is, the more he will be rejected, and the lonelier he will become.

But how do we know that training in communication skills will help? The evidence comes from several sources.

Psychologists have long been interested in the conveying of emotions, an essential ingredient in satisfactory communication. So much research has been done in this area that the results are complicated, and frequently contradictory (Tagiuri, 1969, 404). Sometimes women are better judges of emotion, sometimes men are, sometimes no sex differences are found. Sometimes facial expressions are the best medium for understanding, while vocal cues predominate in other situations. Usually people were better judges of people familiar to them, but even this was not always true.

Despite all the conflicting results, several guidelines for effective communication do exist, which Knapp (1972, 127) summarizes. Heading his list is the suggestion that if we want someone to be adept at judging people's emotions, we train him specifically in that skill. Practiced judges do indeed perform at a higher level than do novices (Davitz, 1964, 20; Guilford, 1929).

Mark Snyder's research at Stanford University (1974) is also relevant here. He discovered that professional stage actors, who presumedly have received direct training in the conveying of emotion, are especially adept at monitoring nonverbal messages.

Delaney (1968, 315) notes that when counselors and other mental health professionals are learning their craft, ". . . training for greater awareness and accuracy in the perception of nonverbal cues increases such sensitivity."

25

Most fundamentally, however, we simply have faith that anything that is learned can be taught. Since much of our nonverbal communication repertoire is learned behavior, it is subject to additional learning, and improvement.

The lonely child cannot easily learn communication skills in the ways most people do—indirectly, tangentially, through casual imitation and observation. We believe that direct instructional intervention—including a great deal of practice—may fill in some of the gaps.

REFERENCES

Birdwhistell, Ray. *Kinesics and Context*. Philadelphia: University of Pennsylvania Press, 1970.

Brammer, Lawrence M. *The Helping Relationship: Process and Skills*. Englewood Cliffs, N.J.: Prentice-Hall, 1973.

Davitz, J. R. *The Communication of Emotional Meaning*. New York: McGraw-Hill, 1964.

Delaney, D. "Sensitization to Non-Verbal Communications." *Counselor Education and Supervision* 7 (1968): 315–316.

Dion, K., and Berscheid, E. "Physical Attractiveness and Sociometric Choice in Nursery School Children." Unpublished paper, 1971. Cited in E. Aronson, *The Social Animal*. San Francisco: W. H. Freeman and Co., 1978, p. 216.

Ekman, P., and Friesen, W. V. "The Repertoire of Non-Verbal Behavior: Categories, Origins, Usage, and Coding." *Semiotica* 1 (1969): 49–98.

Fantz, R. L. "Pattern Vision in Newborn Infants." *Science* 140 (1963): 296–297.

Guilford, J. P. "An Experiment in Learning to Read Facial Expressions." *Journal of Abnormal Social Psychology* 24 (1929): 191–202.

Haggard, E. A., and Isaacs, K. S. "Micromomentary Facial Expressions as Indicators of Ego Mechanisms in Psychotherapy." In L. A. Gottschalk and A. H. Auerbach, eds., *Methods of Research in Psychotherapy*. New York: Appleton-Century-Crofts, 1966, pp. 154–165.

Hall, Edward T. *The Hidden Dimension*. Garden City, N.Y.: Doubleday and Co., 1966.

Harrison, R. P. *Beyond Words: An Introduction to Nonverbal Communication.* Englewood Cliffs, N.J.: Prentice-Hall, 1974.

Kiesler, S., and Baral, R. "The Search for a Romantic Partner: The Effects of Self-Esteem and Physical Attractiveness on Romantic Behavior." n.d. Cited in Ellen Berscheid and Elaine Walster, *Interpersonal Attraction.* Reading, Mass.: Addison-Wesley, 1969, pp. 113–114.

Knapp, Mark L. *Non-Verbal Communication in Human Interaction.* New York: Holt, Rinehart and Winston, 1972.

Snyder, Mark. "The Self-Monitoring of Expressive Behavior." *Journal of Personality and Social Psychology* 30 (1974): 526–537.

Tagiuri, R., "Person Perception." In E. Aronson and G. Lindzey, eds., *The Handbook of Social Psychology.* 2nd ed. Reading, Mass.: Addison-Wesley, 1969, pp. 395–449.

Trager, G. L. "Paralanguage: A First Approximation." *Studies in Linguistics* 13 (1958): 1–12.

Walster, Elaine, Aronson, V., Abrahams, D., and Rottmann, L. "Importance of Physical Attractiveness in Dating Behavior." *Journal of Personality and Social Psychology* 5 (1966): 508–516.

PART 2

Some Possible Causes of Poor Social Perception

The only thing we can say with certainty about faulty social perception is that it exists. Our job is twofold: We must begin to correct nonverbal communication problems directly (Part IV attempts to do just that); and, simultaneously, we must endeavour to understand and to reduce the many possible causes.

Some of the reasons for faulty social perception are discussed in this part. They are grouped under four broad categories: atypical thinking and learning styles, behavioral problems, emotional problems, and perceptual difficulties. Each of these is further subdivided so that a set of well over a dozen different traits (or symptoms) emerge.

This strategy of categorization is done purely so that we can focus upon one characteristic at a time. The actual behavior of human beings is far more complex than any system of classification. In reality, the traits, treated here individually, overlap, one frequently mirroring—or at least contributing to—another. More often than not, several of them occur simultaneously.

For example, relentless talkativeness can be seen as a function of impulsivity, excitability, as well as of perseveration. Failure to listen to—and to become interested in—others is a reflection of egocentricity, is fed by anxiety, and reinforced by poor self-concept. ("I'm so unworthy that we couldn't possibly be friends, anyway.") Excessive interruption can occur because of perceptual deficit (one does not perceive that the other wishes to continue speaking), perseveration (one simply can't stop talking), anxiety, and egocentricity.

Egocentricity is tied in with concretism (the concept of "me" is highly concrete), distractibility (not paying attention to the other person), and poor incidental learning (one has not learned to function in a sociocentric way). It can also contribute to inadequate generalization ability. (After all, if the child is locked into himself in all situations, then he does not deal with those generalizations that involve others.)

To complicate the picture still further, the child is a growing—and changing—organism. Therefore, studying each trait individually has merit only if we remember that we are dealing with the "whole child," and if we couple the knowledge gained from words written about children with direct experiences in observing them and working with them.

CHAPTER 3

Atypical Thinking and Learning Styles

PECULIARITIES IN REASONING

(The setting: an army barracks in a basic training camp. Two recently arrived soldiers are "rapping.")

SOLDIER FROM THE CITY: Hey, what's the matter with you guys from the country? I hear all of you go around making love to sheep and cows and horses and chickens.

SOLDIER FROM THE COUNTRY:[Incredulously]: *Chickens???*

That's an old joke, probably of World War II vintage. The unexpected response is what comes across as funny. Our country soldier, by denying one of the charges, without realizing it has tacitly confessed to the others.

This type of peculiarity in reasoning (or at least, in conversing) —selectively addressing oneself to only one of a series of points— can occur for various reasons. It can be a way of fighting back: "Look at you. I'm ashamed to admit you're my daughter. You're overweight, your hair is uncombed, your posture is terrible, you didn't button your blouse properly, your face is dirty, and your slip is showing." "I did so comb my hair, Mother." By catching the parent in one misstatement—a trivial one at that—the child lashes back, but it is a feeble blow, at best.

It can serve as a defense mechanism. "Why don't you have any guts? For heaven's sake, go speak to your adviser and insist that he change your program. Just look at the schedule you arranged for yourself. Three days a week, you have to be in college from 8 A.M. to 8 P.M. On Tuesday, you have only twenty minutes for lunch. Why did you arrange so many huge blocks of free time? You'll never be able to spend them productively—you'll just be groggy. To make it worse, you scheduled your hardest subject, college mathematics, the last part of the day when you'll be the tiredist." "I don't mind having twenty minutes for lunch." By negating the one charge, the individual hopes to lessen the impact of the array of criticism that has been hurled against him. This, too, is ineffective.

It may ensue simply because one does not see the point: "You know, accidents happen more frequently than you might imagine. And most of them can be prevented. All electric cords should be checked for fraying. If the power ever goes off, use flashlights instead of candles. Don't leave things like shoes and toys in the middle of the floor. Never carry sharp objects like compasses, open knives, things made out of glass, or scissors in your pocket. Clear ice and snow off the sidewalk." "Some glass objects aren't sharp." Here, an attempt is made to continue the conversation, but the total essence of what the speaker has said is missed.

Whatever its psychodynamics, this style of responding to a select—almost random—point of a gestalt comes across as bizarre, ineffective, and illogical.

Peculiarities in reasoning can result from many sources. The mentally retarded do not have sufficient intellectual capacity to reason properly. Others, while not retarded, may be intellectually careless. Still others—recently called dyslogic (Wacker, 1975)—despite average to higher intellectual potential, may evidence faulty logic that stems from their brain's inability to compute incoming data correctly and to "print out" logical responses and reactions.

Finally, there are individuals whose emotional maladjustments create feelings of negativism and hostility often coupled with low self-esteem. These are channeled into specific conversational roles (Siegel, 1974, 33–35): the perennial devil's advocate, the constant "straight man," the self-deprecator, the profuse apologizer, and so forth. Impulsivity is another factor. To the extent that logic can be defined as the consequence of thought, the individual who seems impelled to speak (or act) instantaneously without an iota of deliberation is often illogical. If impulsivity is coupled with poor self-concept, the stage is set for a very special kind of illogic—that which is accompanied by stubbornness. It works this way: In the middle of a conversation, with no mulling over and making no effort to preplan (that is, to envision the possible effects of his statement upon others or to estimate the reasonableness of what he is about to say), the impulsive individual, seizing the floor by interrupting, and in a loud, excitable voice, states his position. It is not well-thought-out and hence completely vulnerable to criticism. But, try as they might, the others cannot shake him. Their reasoning is met with total imperviousness. He simply repeats—not even rephrases—his original pronouncement. In short, impulsivity resulted in the original, poorly conceived outburst; poor self-concept (one must feel "big" enough to alter his views publicly) prevented him from modifying his stand.

Some individuals speak in clichés, employing small talk in lieu of reasoned responses. They frequently make conversation for conversation's sake. They may not sense from others' moods that silence is in order, or perhaps some degree of tension contributes to their talkativeness. At any rate, they frequently talk unnecessarily. For example, suppose three high school acquaintances are conversing. The first says that he had to see the principal yesterday. The second relates that only last week she had to report to the assistant principal. The third then blurts out, "The principal is higher than the assistant principal." Obviously, *it goes without saying* that the principal is higher. *But he said it,* and that is the crux of his problem. He says the obvious, the totally gratuitous, that which does not have to be said. Of course, impulsivity can again be a contributor in that the individual is helpless to prevent the fleeting thought from reaching the verbalizing stage.

Reasoning is dependent upon one's capacity for organizing, for making long-range plans, for internalizing past events, perceptions, and conceptions and to use these in formulating current thoughts, vocalizations, and courses of action. Possibilities must be distinguished from probabilities. Degrees of difference and shades of meaning must be perceived. Hypotheses must be formulated and reformulated in the light of new evidence. Results must be anticipated. Clearly the "now" child, regardless of raw intelligence, is at a distinct disadvantage with respect to this "pausing, outlining, and weighing" prerequisite of reasoning.

Certainly social perception is intimately linked with reasoning ability. If one cannot interpret a frown, he misses the message of discontent. If the biting tone of sarcasm escapes him (e.g., "Tommy, you sure are a winner"), he has no way to perceive the real message of disapproval. Quite apart from one's poor capacity for appraisal of nonverbal communication, social judgment is also related to one's reasoning capabilities. It is wrong, that is, *illogical,* to tell jokes and laugh loudly at funerals, to dress sloppily when applying for a job, or to berate the janitor of a supermarket because it overprices.

At times, then, peculiarities in reasoning *stem* directly from inadequacies in social perception (inability to read another's moods, deficits in judging social situations, and so on). In other instances, they *contribute* to faulty social perception. After all, if one's brain does not decode sensory input properly nor encode appropriate responses, if one responds to only a single aspect of a gestalt and ignores its totality, if an individual's emotional and/or perceptual idiosyncrasies lead him to make illogical self-demeaning remarks, to apologize when no apology is needed, constantly to play the role of "Moishe Kapoyr" (a Yiddish mythical character who invariably takes the opposite point of view), if he frequently assumes an oddball position and holds onto it at all costs, or if he dispenses gratuitous statements profusely, then that person's company—to put it mildly—will not be pursued with any degree of vigor.

One way to become more adept at socializing and learn how to respond logically is to participate in numerous social experiences. But the inability to socialize acceptably leads to further rejection, thus seriously depleting the supply of self-correcting input and consequently robbing the child of opportunities for improvement and trapping him in a vicious cycle.

EGOCENTRICITY

It is developmentally normal for young children to be "locked in" to themselves, and to progress in sociocentric thinking—and language—as they grow older. Egocentric speech can be characterized by lack of concern with whether or not the "listener" is listening, excessive talkativeness, talking about one's self or one's own concerns, ignoring the mood of the listener and failing to identify his lack of receptivity to conversation, and saying things that will make sense only if the listener has had identical experiences (for example, "Billy is a real nice guy" is meaningless if the listener has no idea who Billy is). The egocentric individual makes and repeats assertions rather than justifies them, fails to modify his pronouncements in the light of probable impact upon—and feedback from—the audience, and interrupts frequently. Above all, his speaking style is characterized by the complete absence of any feeling for the *collaboration* aspect of conversation. It is, in fact, only a step away from the extremely young child who talks to himself at play, using language—specifically the naming function of words—merely to help hold onto new perceptions as they are in the process of being formed, sequenced, and stored. In short, the young child thinks and/or talks egocentrically even when "communicating" with others, while the adult thinks sociocentrically, even when alone (Piaget, 1948, 40).

If, for some reason, the child, though chronologically ready for sociocentric functioning (generally thought to be after the age of seven), continues to be basically egocentric, then of course he will not readily receive nonverbal communication cues. How can he? He doesn't even look for them!

It is not uncommon for an egocentric child to yearn for companionship, yet to be sorely lacking in his capacity to "make friends." His self-preoccupation or, more precisely, his "self-boundness" renders him unable to become truly interested in others. Even after the egocentric child has learned to converse in a

37

more relaxed and smoother manner and is capable of displaying a modicum of social amenities, the tenor of what he says remains fixed at the surface level. Clichés abound. It inevitably becomes clear to a potential companion that the "listener" is, in fact, not listening. There is too much talking about "me," no catering to —indeed, no awareness of—the other's feelings. It is axiomatic that each of us, regardless of age and irrespective of our degree of emotional and social adjustment, never outgrows the basic need for acceptance and for feelings of belonging, uniqueness, and importance. But the egocentric person is unable to give us the positive "strokes" we seek and this generates negative reactions in us. In a sort of psychological retaliation (at a subconscious level), we respond in kind by rejecting the source of our discomfort. This phenomenon of imitative reaction is not uncommon. Doesn't anger beget anger? Don't we tend to like others if they like us? Aren't such mood indicators as humor, relaxation, and nervousness contagious? Hence egocentricity accounts for one being bored as well as boring. And the irony of it all is that the egocentric's inability to feel and to show concern for others in no way minimizes his *need* for others. In short, he is alone by virtue of his language and thinking style, by his immature level of social development, and by his very personality—but not by choice.

CONCRETISM

An overly concrete style in thinking and in using language can cause one to miss many of the nuances and subtleties in conversation. Certainly, the words themselves are more concrete than are the accompanying nonverbal cues. Hence, the overly literal person hears "You really are a genius," but misses the sarcasm. "Are you quite done?" registers simply as a neutral question, but the real message of impatience goes unnoticed. A superficial "How are you?" mumbled almost in passing can become an open invitation for a complete oral inventory of life's recent vagaries and for biographical events in general.

Even verbal messages have shades of meaning that can be lost if taken out of context. Idioms abound that further handicap the overly literal individual. "Fat chance" and "slim chance" mean the same. "Flammable" and "inflammable" are identical. "Slow up" and "slow down" have synonymous, not opposite meanings. In the field of public relations, "coverage" and "exposure" lose their antonym relationship. "Invaluable" means *more* than valuable despite the prefix *in* (not). "You could have knocked me over with a feather," "My head was spinning," "My stomach was tied up in knots," "He was scared out of his skin," are not to be taken literally. One educator relates an anecdote of a pupil who was asked to punch a hole in a piece of paper. He made the hole with the hole-puncher—and then proceeded to punch it with his fist!

There is yet another aspect of concrete thinking that hinders social effectiveness. Pure concretism deals with the "here and now" only, whereas the ability to abstract entails the concept of past and future as well. Concrete thinking is limited to only those things and events that can be experienced sensorially; more mature conceptualization involves planning, insight, imagination, and the manipulation of hypothetical constructs. The overly concrete individual is bound to things rather than to ideas, to gross concepts rather than to nuances, to what *is* rather than what *could* be.

Finally, the utterances of the concrete person are generally characterized by superficiality and are markedly devoid of in-depth *feeling*. It is not so much a question of which of the two—words or feelings—are more abstract. After all, a good case can be made that since feelings began developing prior to spoken language, they are more primitive, more basic, more *concrete*. Most likely, what is operating here is that the very notion that words can be used to convey emotions is too abstract for the concrete individual to grasp.

There is, of course, a strong relationship between concretism and egocentricity. In fact, egocentricity can be seen as the epitome of concretism: What can be more concrete than "me"?

Clearly, the individual who focuses totally upon the spoken word while missing the accompanying nonverbal communication, who has not grasped the subtleties of idioms and who does not discern shades of meaning, who is limited to the "here and now" and who is utterly lacking in imagination comes across as immature, uninteresting, and "different." Rejection occurs. Loneliness ensues. And the very experience—that is, socialization—that can enable the overly concrete child to move toward a greater capacity for handling abstractions is denied him.

DIFFICULTIES IN MAKING GENERALIZATIONS

The ability to generalize, to discern basic similarities while ignoring trivial differences, can be applied to objects (pencils, pens, crayons, and chalk are all writing implements), people (foremen, supervisors, directors, and coordinators are all bosses), and events (loss of a job, death or illness of a loved one, damage to one's home or automobile, an unsuccessful interview are all sad "happenings").

Our capacity for learning is directly related to our ability to form adequate concepts—that is, to classify, to categorize, to systematize, to organize. This ability enables us to grasp rules and principles and to get the gist of a lecture, a cartoon, a conversation, a social situation. Without it, each occurrence would be unique, would have no relation to any past one, and hence, the individual would be unable to benefit from his various experiences. Doesn't the automobile mechanic, from his experiences with *some* automobiles, make generalizations on the basis of this experience, and later, apply what he has learned to *all* cars? Similarly, the English student learns the definition of parts of speech, in *general*. He later applies his concepts to specific cases and so is able to classify correctly nouns, verbs, adverbs, and so on.

The development of these kinds of concepts equip the individual with the prowess for coping with the multitudes of variations—and frequently, changing variations, at that—existing in his environment. The number of sights, sounds, and other sensory data (not to mention the vast array of thoughts, memories, and feelings) impinging upon him is incalculable. The organism simply could not function were it not for his capacity to make generalizations. Because he can discern similarities beneath divergence, he can organize large chunks of the outside world (Humphrey, 1944, 37). He can assign a sense of stability and continuity to the free-flowing mass of sensory and perceptual data he experiences. He can substitute order for chaos. He can survive.

The facility with which we learn to generalize is linked to our ability to perceive the "whole" instead of getting sidetracked by its parts. If one's perceptual mechanism is such that parts rather than wholes, and background rather than foreground are generally emphasized, then the *essence* of the perceptual event is missed. Clearly, the likelihood that the individual will be able to make the necessary conceptual transfer from one situation to another is rendered virtually nil since he did not even grasp the main point of the *original* stimulus.

For example, Charlotte is being interviewed for a job as a clerk-typist in a law office. Mr. Jones, the prospective employer, has a large collection of leather-bound books. The wall-to-wall bookcase is directly in back of his chair (which is also made of leather). Throughout the interview, Charlotte is fascinated by the luxurious chair, by the abundance of books, and by the very notion that books and chairs can be made of the same material. Simultaneously, she begins to answer his question regarding her past work experiences. After some time, Mr. Jones pauses, stands, smiles, and says, "It was very nice to meet you. We have to see two more applicants, then we'll contact you early next week to let you know our decision." But Charlotte, sidetracked by the surroundings as well as her own intruding thoughts, misses this cue and continues to bombard the listener with additional data regarding her qualifications.

It is safe to say that her inability to perceive—and hence to attend avidly rather than perfunctorily—to the foreground of this event, hurt her chances of landing the job. Moreover, since she missed the original point, she cannot even begin to generalize an essential relationship—namely, when the interviewer pauses, stands, and gives verbal as well as nonverbal signals that he has finished, the interview is over. Because she does not benefit by experience, she will probably continue to be unsuccessful in all social situations coming under the broad heading of "interviews": with other prospective employers, with college advisers, with bank loan officers, with employment counselors, and the like.

Rigidity is another trait that militates against the development of adequate generalizing ability. The prime symptom of rigidity (or perseveration) is that the individual deals entirely with the immediate sensory data and refuses (is unable?) to abandon it long enough to consider what follows. But generalizing implies some degree of perceptual and conceptual flexibility; that is, elements of a "whole" must frequently be regrouped to accommodate new situations. Consider the following parlor game: Ask someone how would a deaf-mute communicate to a hardware clerk that he wants to buy a hammer. Answer? By pantomiming. Next ask how would a foreigner let the storekeeper know that he wants to buy a saw. Answer? Once more, pantomiming. Then ask how would a blind man apprize the clerk of his desire to purchase a pair of scissors? The individual may again reply, "by pantomiming," completely overlooking the fact that blind people can talk. If a mental set is formed too quickly and held onto too tightly, the obvious will go unnoticed. (As the "pantomiming" riddle shows, the average person also forms mental sets too quickly on occasion, but learning disabled individuals are more prone to such errors and may require more detailed explanations before they see how they have gone wrong.)

Besides inadequacies in dealing with wholes instead of parts, foreground-background confusion, and a tendency toward rigidity in thinking, additional characteristics contribute to meager skills in generalizing. For example, the egocentric is too self-bound to deal significantly with any perceptual data involving others: After Jack's first day in junior high school, he meets his friend Helen. He begins to describe his new teachers to her in detail. Helen is in a hurry to get home because she is worried about her sick mother. Jack continues talking, not noticing Helen's furrowed brow, downturned corners of mouth, wringing hands, and nervous weight shifting. She tries to get a word in edgewise, but the stream of his utterances is unrelenting. He is in the middle of a sentence, when, in desperation, she turns and walks away blurting out, "I'm sorry. I have to go now." Even if Jack possesses the perceptual ability to interpret Helen's nonverbal signals, his egocentricity prevents him from taking notice of them.

Concretism boxes one in too completely with the present, seriously reducing the likelihood that past events or future possibilities will be considered: It is a rainy day. Maria is showing her new two-wheeled bicycle to two of her friends who have come to her home to visit. At first, they are extremely interested in it. After some time, Margaret and Helen begin reminiscing about their first tricycles, and later still, the conversation shifts to driving cars when they are older. Maria does not contribute to either of these themes, but continues, inappropriately, to inject statements about her bicycle. Margaret and Helen, irritated by Maria's uninteresting conversational offerings (that is, by this unyielding harping upon the "here and now"), cut short their visit and leave in the rain.

Passivity reduces normal curiosity and can hold to a minimum any deliberation regarding such concepts as cause-effect relationships: Henry generally seems to be preoccupied. He is not assertive and tends to accept events without question. (To question would mean to intervene, to participate, to assert, and even to confront—and Henry is not so inclined.) Even his speech is lethargic and comes out as a mumble. People frequently fail to answer him. They "step on his lines." They misunderstand him. For example, Henry says, "I'm *hungry*," and his friend responds, "What are you *angry* about?" Henry doesn't bother to inform his friend that he isn't angry nor to inquire what was it that gave him that idea. Instead, he simply shrugs his shoulders.

Thus it is apparent that many factors can play a role in diminishing one's ability to generalize. Equally important is the fact that this deficit in generalizing skills assumes a momentum of its own and takes its toll in other areas. Certainly, social acumen is inextricably bound to the ease with which you make generalizations. A frown signifies disapproval no matter who is doing the frowning and regardless of the circumstances. Raised eyebrows means that the "speaker" is puzzled, is contemplating, does not fully grasp, etc. This quizzical expression has the same meaning whether in response to a spoken question, studying a painting, or perusing a menu. If you do not generalize adequately or accurately, you will miss many of these nonverbal messages. You will subsequently come across as "different" and your social acceptability will be lessened.

The lonely child whose poor social perception stems from difficulty in making generalizations is rendered even less effective by the ensuing rejection. This situation is like that of an individual who commits a crime. Imprisonment is the result, and this in itself makes it more likely that his criminality will increase.

DEFECTIVE INCIDENTAL LEARNING SKILLS

Since all learning is important, it is fruitless to debate which kind of learning—intentional or incidental—is more necessary. Moreover, even in an "intentional learning" setting (that is, a classroom lesson), the superior learner, in addition to garnering those ideas and skills that the teacher imparts, is simultaneously learning tangential points. In a lesson involving multiplication, if the teacher uses the term "seven times five," as well as simply "seven fives," the able student soon sees that these expressions are interchangeable *even though the teacher did not make a point of this.* A lesson on rhyming may merely stress that the last part of the words "from the vowel to the end" must be the same. The gifted student may then perceive, *with no instructions from the teacher,* that in words of more than one syllable, the accent is a factor also: *recent* and *descent* do not rhyme despite the fact that they end the same.

Incidental learning is a function of memory. For example, in a psychological study the subject may be told to put the big toy airplane next to the little one, the big ball next to the small one, the big car next to the small one. Later, when the toys are out of view, he is asked to recall their colors.

Your ability to learn incidentally is also dependent upon your peripheral perception. When paying attention to the foreground, can you still note some details of the background? For example, when a pupil is solving a long division example in his notebook, does he simultaneously—*and without any cues from the teacher*—take into account the amount of remaining page space and the size of his writing? Having been assigned coat-hook number sixteen, does he recognize within several days the "neighboring" classmates who have numbers fifteen and seventeen? After the teacher has located Oregon on a large wall map of North America and has carried on a class discussion of it with the map in view, has the pupil noticed *without any instruction* that this state touches the Pacific Ocean and is near Canada? After singing "The Star Spangled Banner" daily for several years, has the pupil learned, simply by listening and via kinesthetic cues (the "feeling" in his voice apparatus), that the words *glare* in the line "and the rocket's red glare" and *free* just before the end of the first stanza are the highest notes of that melody? In some instances, the peripheral stimuli will literally be on the periphery of the foreground. In other cases, they may be imbedded in it, but they are still on the periphery of the *topic* under focus. In either case, the key question is whether or not you can note subordinate data while attending to the main point.

Incidental learning involves not only the recording of mere sensory data, but also entails seeing relationships. Many motorists, *without any outside instruction,* have learned to stay in lane by straddling the dark "exhaust line." Some restaurant-goers in New York City have figured out that by doubling the eight-percent sales tax on a bill, they can quickly approximate the waiter's tip of fifteen percent. A young child soon learns that if he doesn't want the drinking fountain to splash him, he'd better turn on the faucet slowly and not all the way.

Certainly incidental learning is dependent to a large degree upon intelligence. In fact, highly intelligent children who are also highly creative, often learn best by themselves. E. Paul Torrance (1962, 5) points out:

> . . . the highly creative child appears to learn . . . without appearing to work . . . hard. . . . These highly creative children are learning and thinking when they appear to be "playing around." Their tendency is to learn creatively more effectively than by authority. They may engage in manipulative and/or exploratory activities, many of which are discouraged or even forbidden. They enjoy learning and thinking, and this looks like play rather than work.

Absence of tension is another prerequisite for the development of incidental learning prowess. After all, if anxiety, depression, phobias, and self-preoccupation can drain your attention from the *task at hand,* then certainly they make it even more unlikely that you will record, retrieve, and use productively *peripheral* sensory

45

data. Similarly, self-esteem is a necessary ingredient. The child beset with self-doubts and having a poor self-concept feels that "I'm not important and neither are my ideas, my thoughts, my discoveries." If nothing matters, why bother to learn, intentionally or incidentally?

Some authors have stated that although mentally retarded individuals have difficulty with incidental learning, they will be able to learn incidentally as long as the teacher calls peripheral data to their attention and points out the relationship of this data to other events and stimuli they are experiencing (Smith, 1974, 102). The semantic flaw here is obvious: The moment the teacher calls explicit attention to those elements of the child's environment that ordinarily should be absorbed by him independently, then it is no longer *incidental* learning. The point is, though, that retardates—as well as those who, though not retarded, may still evidence some kind of learning problem (for example, the learning disabled, the emotionally disturbed, and the unmotivated)—*can learn, provided they are taught.* And so can the many lonely children who are socially imperceptive. Although the vast majority acquire social perception via experience, observation, feedback, and trial and error, those who do not readily learn in this manner *can be taught specifically what others are able to learn tangentially.* For them to be able to make the proper judgments regarding the actions and intents of those with whom they come in contact, we must *teach* them to interpret facial expressions, to read messages of gesture, to understand the hidden meanings of vocal inflections, to grasp the significance of personal and social space, and even to *express* themselves appropriately using nonverbal communication.

However, there will always be unique situations, novel settings, and unfamiliar combinations of events in any child's life. Specific instructions cannot prepare him for these. Therefore, although most of the remedial activities included in Part 4 offer explicit instruction in receiving and delivering nonverbal communication signals, many of them also provide direct training in extending peripheral perception, short-term memory, seeing relationships, making generalizations, and so forth. While strengthening the child's social perception, these activities nurture his incidental learning skills.

REFERENCES

Humphrey, George. "The Problem of Generalization." *Bulletin of Canadian Psychological Association,* 4, no. 3 (October 1944): 37–51.

Piaget, Jean. *The Language and Thought of the Child.* London: Routledge and Kegan Paul, 1948.

Siegel, Ernest. *The Exceptional Child Grows Up.* New York: E. P. Dutton, 1974.

Smith, Robert M. *Clinical Teaching.* 2nd ed. New York: McGraw-Hill, 1974.

Torrance, E. Paul. *Guiding Creative Talent.* Englewood Cliffs, N.J.: Prentice-Hall, 1962.

Wacker, John. "The Dyslogic Syndrome." In *Texas Key,* state newsletter of the Association for Children with Learning Disabilities, September 1975.

CHAPTER 4

Behavioral Problems

PERSEVERATION

Scene I

ALICE: I think Barbra Streisand is a tremendous singer. She is a great actress and a really good comedienne.

MABEL: Elvis Presley was my favorite. He could sing a lot of different kinds of songs. He was great with rhythm songs and his "Love Me Tender" was nice and sweet.

ALICE: She sure can do things with volume. She really belts out the loud notes, and her soft ones are clear, they don't "quiver" at all and they're so soft that you're amazed you can hear them.

Scene II

FRED: I think George Washington was the greatest president we ever had. He was an excellent military man, too. Since he was first, he could not look back to any past presidents and profit by their mistakes.

BOB: I think Lincoln was the best. Of course his main idea was to save the Union. But, by his Emancipation Proclamation, he ended slavery before any other president would have.

FRED: Franklin D. Roosevelt was also a great president. He pulled us out of a terrible depression and got us to all stick together during the war.

BOB: With all that Watergate business, I know Nixon is unpopular now. But as time goes by, I think people will realize he did some very good things, too. He was the only one who could have made détente with Russia and with China. The conservatives would have chewed up McGovern.

ANNA: Hey. Did you guys hear the latest news? I saw it on TV. Nixon just resigned. He was saying good-bye to his staff. He was crying and . . .

FRED: I like Harry S. Truman. He was a salty guy. He told it like it was. He had the guts to do what he thought was right.

Scene III

JACK: How do you like school this term?

HARRY: Great. I'm really catching onto algebra. I do well on the problems as well as the examples. In fact, I got ninety-five on my last test. I find French easier than I thought I would. I don't think my accent is good, but I catch on to the grammar OK. We have an excellent teacher in social studies. He gets us to think and is very interesting himself. My English teacher loves literature and her enthusiasm makes the classes important to me. I never was good in gym but I kind of like shooting baskets. The food is getting worse this year. We have a new principal . . . etc., etc., etc.

In each of these scenes, one of the characters is an ineffective conversationalist. In Scene I, Alice is talking about Barbra Streisand throughout. So compelled is she to continue with her own thoughts that she totally ignores Mabel's nomination of Elvis Presley. In Scene II, Fred and Bob are discussing the merits of various presidents. Fred is completely locked into the format, namely, two characters—he and Bob—are taking turns voicing their opinions. This has become so ritualized for Fred that when Anna—a third party—interjects some extremely exciting news, he pays absolutely no attention to her and continues instead with the original pattern: my turn, Bob's turn, my turn, Bob's turn, my turn, etc. In Scene III, Harry gives an overly long response to a question that logically demands only a perfunctory answer.

49

All of these scenes have something in common: The "transgressors" are not flexible. Once started, they do not stop. They go on and on. They *perseverate*.

Perseveration has been defined as the tendency to continue with an activity long after there is any logical need to do so. The perseverative person has been likened to a phonograph needle that gets stuck in one groove of the record, playing that portion over and over and over again. A classic example of perseveration is to continue to pound a nail, even after it has gone all the way into the wood. Such action is not bizarre. It was once appropriate; its inappropriateness lies in its continuous repetition (Siegel, 1961, 19). Comedy writers have always recognized the oddity of such behavior. Remember Charlie Chaplin knocking on the door and continuing the knocking motion even after the door was opened? We've all heard comedy routines in which a punch line is developed early and then repeated relentlessly at strategic points throughout the entire act.

In many instances, perseveration is linked with neurological handicap (often minimal in degree) whereby the individual, because of perceptual impairment, finds it difficult to integrate the myriad sensory stimuli that besiege him into meaningful, "whole" patterns. Therefore, when he finally does structure a set of incoming data, he seems reluctant to let it go and begin a new one. He cannot readily shift from one situation to another. So he *perseverates*—continues an activity that he is unable to cease or to modify, although its appropriateness has waned.

By no means is perseveration found only among the neurologically handicapped. When individuals who have been diagnosed as emotionally disturbed behave that way, we call it compulsiveness. Some typical compulsive acts are touching every picket in a fence, deliberately stepping on every crack in the sidewalk, washing hands an excessive number of times daily, even doodling.

Perseveration is perfectly normal in very young children. Some slow learners—those who have the mental age of a younger child—may continue to manifest perseverative behavior. In other words, they have not yet *learned* to be less perseverative. At times, normal people of all ages may be perseverative, particularly under conditions like tension, fear, or prolonged fatigue. Very likely, stress tends to limit your ability to interact *flexibly* with your environment. Hence, instead of confronting and integrating each new set of perceptual events, you deal only with the original one. After all, it requires some degree of alertness and some effort to be able to manipulate abstracts and to reorganize incoming data continually.

It often occurs in children after an initial success: How much is three times five? Fifteen. Right! Now can you tell me how much is four times six? Fifteen. How much is five times seven? Fifteen. Perhaps this is the child's subconscious effort to recapture the feeling of success, which may come relatively infrequently to him.

Perseveration is not a predictable factor. It can occur in a variety of situations and in different forms (Siegel, 1961, 19–20). In writing a word, a perseverative child may suddenly write one letter over and over again. In crayoning, he may cover the entire page with a single color. He may also perseverate at the conceptual level, harping upon earlier ideas instead of going on to more appropriate, current ones, or by carrying over the old "tried and true" meaning of words to all situations, apparently oblivious to the notion that the same word may have several different connotations, *depending upon the context in which it is being used at any given instance.* It may not be a question of intellect. He may simply feel more comfortable—given his perceptual, neurological, and/or emotional makeup—dealing with absolutes, with constancies, with fixed quantities, and with consistent relationships.

Excessive talkativeness can be another characteristic of those given to perseveration. They talk, not so much for the purpose of communication, but simply because they cannot stop talking. They may talk about the same topic incessantly for months at a time. *All* subjects will be "talked to the hilt" rather than receive the cursory attention that some of them deserve. They may ask the same question over and over again even after it is apparent that they know the answer. There are several possible explanations for this type of behavior. Besides those we have mentioned (slow learners have not yet abandoned their childish, perseverative mode of communication; the neurologically impaired, currently called learning disabled, cannot readily organize incoming sensory data into meaningful patterns; those with emotional problems cannot control their obsessive-compulsive behavior), it has been sug-

51

gested that many individuals who present behavioral, social, or learning problems generally receive from *others*—their parents, teachers, friends—patter and trivia rather than in-depth communication. That is, because they are perceived as somewhat odd, others don't really level with them, choosing instead to converse with them only at the surface level (Kronick, 1976, 115–119). Just as "baby talk" begets "baby talk," pseudocommunication begets pseudocommunication.

There are still other ways in which perseveration hinders the emergence of an effective "talking" style. Perseverative individuals become completely absorbed in what they are going to say instead of listening to the speaker, and wait in excruciating impatience to seize the floor. They are notorious interrupters yet, conversely, exhibit a total inability to tolerate even the politest and most smoothly injected interruption by another. They will present their view over and over again, but refuse to modify it or even rephrase it in any attempt to clarify or to persuade. The dialogue (monologue?) is peppered with reiteratives—"I'm saying . . ." "But I mean . . ." etc., which are invariably followed by the exact words that only a moment ago failed to make the point.

There is a clear connection between perseveration and social imperception. A person who is unduly perseverative will usually have a great deal of difficulty in deriving optimal meaning from nonverbal communication signals: If he is in the throes of some perseverative physical act (drumming of fingers, buttoning and unbuttoning of jacket, tapping of foot), then he is not concentrating fully on the speaker and will therefore miss most of the message—nonverbal as well as verbal. If he is talking a subject to death and all his energies go into *his* vocal production, then he literally is not receptive to the other's facial expression, eye movements, and gestures. If he persists in being overly concrete about such phrases as "feet planted firmly on the ground," "on pins and needles," "a frog in my throat," then he will continue to miss the point. And if, during any kind of social interaction, he remains rigid and inflexible with respect to the stream of nonverbal signals being transmitted, he will not bend with changing situations. For example, he may have started out conversing effectively with one individual—but suddenly a third person joins. He may have surmised correctly that an acquaintance with whom he began speaking was in an "up" frame of mind—but all at once this mood has changed. He may have recognized the air of seriousness engendered by his teacher's opening remarks (and manner)—but now her tone becomes more frivolous.

The point is that social situations, especially informal and spontaneous ones, are in constant flux. The individual who cannot organize—*and reorganize*—the array of sensory stimuli impinging upon him gets locked in to the "old" set of messages. His concept formation becomes disturbed and he does not react—that is, doesn't *behave*—in the expected manner. Like the broken record, he is "in the wrong groove."

IMPULSIVITY

The young child typically "wants what he wants when he wants it." He is unwilling—or unable—to postpone gratification. He functions largely from an emotional frame of reference and does not consider the consequences of his actions.

As he matures, he is better able to govern his impulses. The ability to reason heightens and he is able to make proper judgments regarding the efficacy of his *contemplated* actions. He can now stop, envision himself performing some behavior without actually carrying it out, deliberate, decide whether or not the proposed conduct is in his best interests, and then act accordingly. Although all of this is done subconsciously and almost instantaneously, the point is that *it is done*.

A stable individual is not necessarily unemotional; he has emotions but he can *control* their expression. When appropriate, he will react emotionally or impulsively. Watch people on a picket line, at a horse race, at a political convention! But in general, well-adjusted individuals govern their impulses. They ask the right questions: Should I do it? What will happen if I do? What will others think of me? Should I do something else instead? Is it better to do nothing?

A distinction should be made between *uninhibited* and *disinhibited* behavior. Uninhibited individuals are able to perceive the reactions of others to their behavior, but they do not *choose* to inhibit themselves. They frequently come across as "gutsy," out-spoken, and somewhat eccentric. In fact, they are sometimes admired because they are cheeky, open, and have unmitigated (but often, coveted) gall. They "tell it like it is" and "let it all hang out." With the *disinhibited,* on the other hand, it is not a matter of choice. They often cannot perceive the reaction of society to their behavior and cannot check themselves. They may wish desperately to be accepted and would gladly obey all the rules, if only they could.

There is a "driven" quality to impulsivity (Siegel, 1961, 38, 39). Send a young, impulsive, disinhibited child upstairs for a handkerchief, he will race all the way, fling open the drawer, scatter its contents, and return with a dozen of them. If you tell him to wash his hands and face, he will dart into the bathroom, turn on all the faucets full blast, splash about enthusiastically, wetting the floors, walls, and mirrors; then he will hurry out, much wetter and sometimes even a trifle cleaner. He doesn't walk, he runs. He doesn't close doors, he slams them. He doesn't put his shoes in the closet, he throws them in.

Hyperactivity (excessive movement and activity) is frequently present in such people. This complicates the picture, resulting in actions that are gross and jerky as well as impulsive.

Impulsivity and poor social perception are intimately linked: The driven, disinhibited, hyperactive, impulsive child cannot (or at least, does not) wait long enough to receive and to interpret non-verbal communication cues. Impulsivity goes hand in hand with excitability. The first stimulus—not necessarily the most important one—is enough to set in motion the "out of the blue" behavior. The impulsive child interrupts incessantly for two reasons: (1) he doesn't take the time to read the nonverbal message that clearly states "I haven't finished yet," and (2) he cannot control his urge to speak now. He changes the subject too often and too abruptly. He frequently leaves without saying "good-bye" and begins telephone conversations without the proper amenities. He cannot pay attention to the speaker because he cannot check his own intruding thoughts.

A special, paradoxical kind of loneliness ensues. The impulsive, disinhibited individual—*even when in the midst of others*—is still very much alone. Like the egocentric who is always locked into himself, like the overly concrete individual who constantly misses the point, like the perseverative person who forever is "on the wrong track," the impulsive individual cannot settle down long enough to take into account the points of view of others. He is unable really to converse, that is, to give and take messages. He is totally lacking in the social aspects of communication. He is, in essence, forever on the outside.

DISTRACTIBILITY

Teachers have perennially complained about the distractibility of some children. Attention is considered by many educators and psychologists to be the first prerequisite to learning. Almost all screening tests used to identify high-risk learners include an item dealing with "inattentiveness," "short attention span," and the like. Most teachers can easily recognize attention problems, particularly when they occur in young children, who have not yet learned how to feign attention. Some typical signs are: failing to make eye contact with the speaker, not focusing eyes on the task at hand, talking when others are talking, motor restlessness (fidgeting, fiddling with various objects, not sitting still), appearing not to listen, "losing" the place in reading even when the student is a good reader, not responding when one's name is called, a "faraway" look, being unable to follow instructions, and, of course, giving incorrect answers to questions dealing with points that have been made only a moment ago.

There are different causes for distractibility. Learning disabled individuals have neurological impairment that makes it difficult for them to filter out unimportant sensory data and concentrate on the task at hand. This is no trivial consideration, as a very simple experiment will prove. Even as you read these words, look at the many sights (colors, bright lights, objects) that *could* be capturing your attention. Are there any sounds that, until this moment, you were successful in ignoring? (Outside traffic? Coughs? Scraping of chairs or of feet? Hum of the air-conditioner?) When you think about it, you can suddenly become aware of the pressure of your wristwatch, the weight of your eyeglasses, the tightness of your belt and shoes, the hardness (or softness) of your chair, the feel of this very book you are holding. But why didn't you attend to these stimuli before? The sights, and sounds, and tactile pressures were there all along, but, fortunately, you did not pay attention to them and so were better able to concentrate on the sole task of reading. The learning disabled, however, have a faulty "filtering mechanism" and are at the mercy of *all* the sensory stimuli that continually bombard them. They often pay attention to background data instead of to the foreground (the room, furniture, pictures, other people who may be present instead of the speaker) and to parts instead of wholes (the speaker's ring, his tie, his eyeglasses rather than to what he is saying and—even more importantly—the manner in which he is saying it).

It has been hypothesized (Havighurst, 1966, 19) that some disadvantaged children may simply have inferior *habits* of listening and attending. That is, in their environment, characterized by few opportunities for communicating with adults, they fail to learn how to pay attention to the speaker.

Emotional problems can be another cause for distractibility. Fantasizing and excessive daydreaming militate against attention. Phobias of various kinds also interfere with attention since the child becomes overly concerned with the object of his phobia and sometimes dwells on it to the exclusion of other, more appropriate thoughts. For example, if you are claustrophobic, then it goes without saying that you will not learn anything while you are "fenced in" during a ride in a crowded elevator. More important, if your fear is intense, you may *relive* the episode time and again. This perseverative aspect of phobias makes the child incapable of paying attention to the task at hand. Finally, any undue preoccupation with self keeps him from listening to, and from showing any real interest in others.

Development of social perception demands attention to the total situation. The child must listen to the words themselves while simultaneously receiving and interpreting nonverbal communication cues. Unquestionably, then, distractibility—regardless of its cause—works against the acquisition of social perception. In addition, a display of distractibility is very disconcerting to the speaker. All of us have a basic psychological need to feel that we're interesting, and that we're important. If the only feedback we get is that we're not coming across and that we're being tuned out, feelings of hostility result. We'll think twice before we seek the company of the overly distractible person.

Research (Hebb, 1949) has shown that the mechanism for attention is housed in the reticular system of the brain. This is the primitive portion, the so-called old brain. It is literally an extension of the spinal cord (often called the brain stem) and is embedded deep in the center of the total brain. Hence, it is, anatomically speaking, far removed from the "new brain"—that is, the cortex, the *thinking* portion of the brain. Nevertheless, it is this thinking part of the brain that can ultimately be instrumental in reducing distractibility. Simply put, one can *learn* to pay attention. Cues, structure, sequence, and practice are some of the conditions for learning.

Motivation is extremely important. Even in situations in which background stimuli become almost unbearable, such as the sound of a construction worker's riveting, it is still possible—though difficult—to concentrate on the speaker, *provided one feels that it is imperative to receive the message.* Doesn't the proud parent observing her youngster in a school play notice every movement, every word, every detail of dress and appearance of her child while virtually ignoring everything else on the stage?

Hence, there is a mutual relationship between attention and learning. You must attend to learn, and you can learn to attend.

GUILELESSNESS

Guilelessness is a characteristic of young children. They are, typically, all-trusting. In fact, adults—especially parents—reinforce this trait in them. Undeniably, there is something appealing about a child who looks at you wide-eyed, searchingly, hungry for acceptance, and without pretense. Gullibility can be seen as a form of dependent behavior, and this dependent relationship can well serve the psychological need of the adult: "The child trusts me, so I am trustworthy. The child is weak, so I am strong. The child is unsophisticated, so I am all-knowing. The child needs me, so I have the *power* to satisfy his need." In other words, children can be an ego trip for us. Show them a magic trick, they don't look for explanations or for telltale hints that would destroy the illusion and the belief that we do indeed have magical powers. Tell them a story, they listen intently. Act silly, tell them a joke, or perform some slapstick routine, they'll laugh uproariously and with total approval. We may even equate guilelessness in children with virtue: faith, purity, being unspoiled and untainted with the hard—at times, sordid—realities of life. It is to *our* advantage that the child believe in Santa Claus and that storks deliver babies.

Sophistication comes with maturity. Most children, as they grow older, develop the knack of "seeing through people." No more are they willing automatically to accept others on face value. You can no longer, as the saying goes, sell them the Brooklyn Bridge. They develop the ability of asking (when the occasion warrants it), "What's the catch?" Immaturity itself, then, is a major cause of gullibility.

It can also spring from a poor self-concept. Perhaps, whether consciously or unconsciously, the gullible child *knows* that the neighborhood children are bragging or boasting, but at least they are talking to him (Siegel, 1961, 22). They are laughing at him, but at least they are not ignoring him. Any contact is better than none. Even an adult who is exploited by others may feel that rejection and loneliness are too great a price to pay for "standing up for my rights." Besides, if he holds himself in low esteem, he may feel too weak, too unimportant, too impotent, too unworthy to challenge the exploiter.

Impulsivity can be a contributor. If you plunge right in without thinking, you are apt to make the wrong decision (for example, accepting a job immediately without consideration of the working conditions, falling for confidence men's schemes, even impulse buying). This kind of impulsivity is, in fact, very much related to concrete thinking: *Acting now* is more concrete behavior than deliberating, imagining, envisioning, planning.

Perceptual impairment may be still another reason for gullibility. A child may be exploitable simply because he does not readily deal in "wholes." He fails to perceive the essence of the event. He is sidetracked by the parts. He simply misses the point.

Gullibility is frequently a symptom of nonverbal communication problems. After all, if you cannot interpret messages transmitted unwittingly by the would-be exploiter's gestures, eye movements, facial expressions, and vocal inflections, then you rely solely upon the spoken words and these can easily trick you. If the child cannot grasp the significance of snickers, sneers, whispering, "put down" pantomimes, and incredulous, quizzical expressions, then he will readily miss the true intention of his "friends" and be vulnerable to exploitation. However, gullibility, once established, acquires a momentum of its own—it becomes part of a life-style, a habit, in which the individual doesn't even *look for* nonverbal signs that might belie the spoken word. In short, the gullible individual behaves differently, is perceived as "different," and is not accepted (except in those isolated events in which others communicate with him only when they want to use him). He, thereby, is denied the numbers and kinds of social experiences that could promote improved social perception and diminish gullibility.

REFERENCES

Havighurst, Robert L. "Who Are the Socially Disadvantaged?" In Joe L. Frost and Glenn R. Hawkes, eds., *The Disadvantaged Child*. Boston: Houghton Mifflin, 1966, pp. 15–23.

Hebb, Donald O. *The Organization of Behavior*. New York: Wiley, 1949.

Kronick, Doreen. "The Importance of a Sociological Perspective Towards Learning Disabilities." In *Journal of Learning Disabilities* 9, no. 2 (February 1976): 115–119.

Siegel, Ernest. *Helping the Brain-Injured Child*. Albany, N. Y.: New York Association for the Learning Disabled, 1961.

CHAPTER 5
Emotional Problems

POOR SELF-CONCEPT

The "self" is the heart of each individual's reality. In fact, our very survival, from a psychological point of view, is dependent upon the emergence of some self-concept. Philosophers have always voiced this concern—"Who am I?" "What am I?" "What's the *real* me like?" In varying degrees, we all search to find ourselves, to know ourselves.

The self-image that we succeed in shaping is dependent upon: (1) our judgment of self-worth, (2) others' judgments of—and reaction to—us, and (3) our interpretation of their reaction. If they accept us, we tend to develop a positive self-concept. Conversely, rejection brings negative self-concept, low self-esteem, feelings of inferiority.

In addition, we have a psychological need to have incoming data that is *consistent with our expectations*. Psychologists point out that it is imperative that we *know* ourselves even if we don't like ourselves (Connolly, 1971, 168). It is, of course, more desirable to have both—a well-defined, consistent, familiar self-image as well as high self-esteem. But where both are not readily attainable, it seems that we strive primarily to maintain consistency. Suppose an individual, because his behavior is inconsistent, sometimes—*and only sometimes*—incurs the wrath of others. They convey their disapproval during these episodes verbally and, probably even more so, by nonverbal communication. Consequently, the individual gradually builds up a negative self-concept. Now suppose that, at other times, he behaves appropriately, and the appropriate signals of approval ensue. He misses these, he distorts them, he misreads them. They do not compute. They are at odds with the picture he has of himself. Favorable self-esteem is sacrificed on the altar of congruency.

To make the matter worse, others, too, are "lazy," or at least somewhat rigid, with respect to the impressions they form of him. An impression is formed and held. Any contrary data—in this case, the "normal," acceptable behavior—is ignored since it violates previously formed opinions. There is an undeniable aspect of anticipation. Self-concept as well as opinions regarding the merit and acceptableness of others depend as much upon expectation as they do upon the actual signals transmitted. Mental sets are too readily formed and too easily crystallized. From all standpoints, then, poor self-concept feeds upon itself. The "transgressor" already has two strikes on him. All people concerned—including himself—give him the third strike gratis and hasten to judge him "out."

There are many external signs of poor self-concept. The individual may walk with stooped posture, develop a fishy, clammy handshake, avoid eye contact, and speak in a too highly pitched tone. He may smile too often (perhaps to mask his own feelings of inadequacy or as an effort—almost always ineffective, by the way—to make others like him). He may become accident-prone (in keeping with his guilt feelings) or a school failure (in deference to his low level of expectation). He is generally uncomfortable with compliments, accepts them ungraciously, frequently "talking himself down." He may hesitate too often, be nondecisive, and develop nervous habits including stuttering or stammering. Timidity, shyness, and withdrawal symptoms are common. On the other hand, he may establish nonproductive defense mechanisms such as pontification, stubbornness, clowning, negativism, aggressiveness, and insulting others. He may willingly become the "goat" of the crowd. He wears a visible "kick me" sign—and society is, all too often, ready to oblige.

There is a strong relationship between poor self-concept and nonverbal communication difficulties. Self-image is formed on the basis of perceiving how others respond to us. They respond to us on the basis of how we act, what we say and especially *how* we say it, and also to our appearance including manner of dress. If we read these reactions incorrectly, then there is no signal to change and the status quo becomes fixed.

Research (Tannenbaum, 1956) has shown that extreme attitudes are held onto more rigidly, and therefore are more resistant to change, than are more moderate ones. Therefore, low self-esteem, which is an extreme attitude, feeds on itself and virtually ensures that the individual will continue to misinterpret any signals of approval that may happen to come his way.

Finally, there is a reciprocal relationship between self-perception and social perception. We have already shown how self-concept is shaped by our perception of how others see and react to us. Equally important is the realization that self-image determines our entire behavior style—including communication. *What I am*—or more correctly, *what I think I am*—determines everything I do, everything I say, and especially the manner in which I say it.

"THE FAILURE SYNDROME"

Some degree of failure is inevitable. Not one of us is immune to it. Any endeavor directed toward growth and change, any social interaction, any environmental negotiation—in other words, just plain living—implies that some failure will occur. In fact, a degree of "risk-taking" behavior is often regarded—and rightfully so—as a sign of mental health, good self-image, and goal direction. The proverbs "If you can't stand the heat, stay out of the kitchen" and "You can't win if you don't play" express it well. But even if you were so wary that you made a point of always "staying out of the kitchen," that is, attempted to isolate yourself completely from any possibility of failure, you would still be a failure—but in a different way: The very act of vigilantly seeking to avoid failure, of trying, so to speak, to wrap yourself in cotton batting, in itself signifies failure. After all, behavior characterized by excessive avoidance and withdrawal can hardly be considered positive since it operates against the best interests (self-actualization, realization of potential, and so forth) of the individual. In addition, failure can nurture learning: It spells out in no uncertain terms "where the person is at" with respect to a given instructional task, demonstrates that a particular methodology did not work (and therefore points out to the teacher the need for a different approach), provides feedback data to the individual that might trigger some behavioral change for the better, and can serve as a backdrop by which to measure any future success in that area. Some educators have actually stated that no one can learn until he has experienced failure.

Notwithstanding the "blessings" of failure, it is safe to say that failure experiences have deleterious effects as well. Some of the consequences are immediate and obvious: If you fail the driver's test, you will not be given a driver's license. If you fail to earn a high enough salary, then you must skimp. If you fail a job interview, you don't get the job. If you fail a math test, your grade is lower.

Beyond these immediate results, failure exacts an even higher toll, especially if encountered repeatedly. The most serious penalty that cumulative failure foists upon the individual is poor self-concept. A negative spiral ensues. The individual, already a poor performer, begins to regard himself as a loser, becomes anxious, fails even more grandly, thus corroborating—and lowering still more—his rapidly dwindling self-esteem. School failure is frequently cited as a prime source of poor self-concept. Boyd McCandless (1967, 608) puts it very cogently:

> Since proficiency in important areas is perhaps the most single base for an adequate self-concept, and since school is the number one childhood arena in which proficiency can and should be gained, failure to develop proficiency is disastrous indeed. No words are sufficient to portray the extremity of disaster of school failure.

But other arenas of failure may be even more detrimental: failure in the family, in the community, in the military, vocationally, physically (with respect to health, physique, appearance, and co-ordination), and especially socially. Regardless of the kind of failure encountered, the cumulative effects can be devastating. The individual who is beset with an absolute dearth of successful experiences gradually withdraws, shunning new situations. His normal curiosity diminishes. Anxiety and boredom heighten.

On top of all this, a strange phenomenon occurs. His feelings of inferiority are so great that he doesn't make use of his feedback mechanism, thus closing off a vital channel for learning. Consider the able reader: If there is a typographical error, if he skips a word or a line, if he makes any reading mistake whatsoever, he stops and says, "Hey, this doesn't make sense. Something is wrong. I'll try it again more carefully. After all, I know when a thing makes sense or not." But the disabled reader, having failed so completely and so consistently in the past, *doesn't expect it to make sense to him*. He doesn't even care if it's understandable or not, he just wants to get it over with (Ross, 1976, 121). So when he reads (erroneously), "The boy tripped on the rug and fell all the way down the stars," he doesn't bat an eyelash. He doesn't get the signal to back off and try to see what's wrong. ("Everything's always wrong anyhow, isn't it?") This style, born of self-deprecation ("I'm so unworthy and insignificant that I have no right to expect to understand") and nurtured by tension ("Please, dear God, let's just finish it") hinders his learning in other academic areas and in nonacademic areas as well. Certainly, if a child has failed in social perception repeatedly, he may well give up trying to understand people and to fathom their moods and intentions. Others, of course, will be quick to discern his feeling of inferiority and will probably reinforce it.

Repeated failure goes hand in hand with a trait known by psychologists as "external locus of control." Taken to extremes, the individual *never* sees himself as instrumental in effecting his own destiny. This often causes him to downgrade himself still further since he is emotionally unable to take credit for any of his accomplishments. If he suddenly improves in school, he will attribute it to the fact that the "work was easy." If his batting average goes up, he will say that the pitcher "took it easy" and just lobbed the ball over the plate. If someone seems interested in him as a person, he will surmise that that individual simply is nice to everyone. By consistently viewing others—and never himself—as the sole controller of events concerning him, he fails to make use of a vital aspect of his own intelligence, that which deals with cause-and-effect relationships. This, of course, helps solidify his image of impotence.

Even in instances in which he is correct in his judgment of others' negative feelings about him, there are several alternatives toward which he can be counseled: Try to become friendly with other people. Participate in after-school social and recreational programs. Join the neighborhood scouts, church groups, or Y. Ask an acquaintance to go to the movies with you. Find someone who will go bowling with you. Become active in politics, especially at the community level. Try to find a job or volunteer your services in areas where you can meet others. Pursue some social hobby like square dancing, chess, or arts and crafts. These outlets exist, but one must, of course, opt for them. The trouble with victims of the failure syndrome is that they no longer have the fortitude for exploration, their enthusiasm has waned, their initiative is nil. They're so sure that whatever they try will turn out badly that they find it safer to do nothing and to be lonely.

ANXIETY

Anxiety in the lonely child will probably increase as he grows older—unless some form of intervention occurs. Hence, it is imperative that those who would seek to neutralize the disastrous effects of excessive anxiety view it in all of its dimensions: its causes, its characteristics, its effects, its correlation with other traits such as frustration and poor self-concept, and finally the connection between anxiety, nonverbal communication lacks, and loneliness.

Anxiety exists in varying degrees. If a person lacks all feelings of anxiety—the so-called sociopath—he behaves in a manipulating manner, develops only tenuous ties with others, is incapable of long-range goals, never feels an iota of guilt, frequently comes in conflict with the law, and often does poorly in school—he is out for "number one" only and doesn't worry about whether or not he is liked by his parents, his teachers, or anyone else. The concepts of conscience, guilt, immorality, and sin are alien to him. He can often beat a lie-detector test: He registers no emotions because he doesn't feel any. Such a person may well succeed in tricking others, in shortcuts, in not getting caught, but essentially he is a failure in his own way—he is a loner.

Authorities recognize that some degree of anxiety serves as a strong motivational factor, spurring the individual on to perform, to accomplish, to conform, to "get with it," to succeed.

Anxiety is a prime source of tension—probably synonymous with it. It disturbs emotional equilibrium. When we feel anxious, it is as though a balance spring is stretched. We strive to recapture the normal state of relaxation by studying harder, doing the task that we kept putting off and fretting about, endeavoring to earn more money in order to get rid of worrisome debt, checking to see whether we turned off the gas burner, "talking things out" with the person with whom we had a misunderstanding. These are positive steps. The individual copes with anxiety by changing the environmental factors that caused it. Some people, however, instead of meeting reality head on, develop avoidance behavior coupled with maladaptive psychological defense mechanisms such as denial ("I'm a good reader, but I'm not trying"), rationalization ("I don't have any friends, but it's not important to have friends"), projection ("I can't play with them because they don't know how to play right"), or displaced emotions ("This stupid pencil can't write good—I'll break it").

Frustration is a key component of anxiety (Connolly, 1971, 165). That is, when you are thwarted from reaching your goals, you are "on edge." This very anxiety, if sufficient in magnitude, may then interfere with your memory, your capacity for reasoning, attention, coordination, and performance in general. In trying *too* hard, you virtually ensure failure. Hence, there is a mutual relationship between anxiety and poor performance—one being both the cause and effect of the other.

Many children diagnosed as learning disabled may suffer more than their share of anxiety because of perceptual factors. The normal population is able to shift mental sets to deal effectively with the constant flux of environmental events (for example, changing classes in a departmental program in junior high school, a fire drill, changing of the topic in an informal conversation, the mood changes of people with whom we are talking). We can organize new sensory data into reliable perceptions and act accordingly. Perceptual impairment, however, implies some rigidity. There is simply not enough time to assimilate all incoming data, and so, that individual is said to feel—and to behave—as though in a perennial panic.

Those with emotional problems are often beset with fears and phobias. They are nervous and don't know how to relax. Anxiety is their trademark.

Self-consciousness is another factor. Some children, usually those with past failure experiences and resultant poor self-concept, feel extremely tense when their performance is being evaluated. Being put on the block—especially by teachers and parents—can be extremely threatening to them psychologically. So important is this consideration, that it has been given its own name: *test anxiety* (Sarason *et al.,* 1960).

Indecisiveness is yet another by-product of anxiety—particularly when coupled with feelings of low self-esteem. The anxious individual will offer a giggle instead of a laugh: That's the midpoint between the decision to laugh and not to laugh. Stuttering is sometimes seen as a compromise between an approach (speaking) and avoidance (not speaking). Similarly, a weak handshake is a compromise between not shaking hands and shaking hands firmly. Tension is contagious. Don't we get nervous if people around us are tense? To carry this further, we don't *like* to feel nervous and, therefore, are bound to react negatively (at least, at the subconscious level) toward the source of our discomfort.

Children who have learning, behavioral, or social problems often generate anxiety in their parents. The parents' anxiety subsequently feeds into that of the child, thus creating a vicious cycle.

Although from a developmental point of view anxiety about yourself or others evolves even before language, language is the medium by which you can learn to understand, handle, and ultimately to lower your anxiety. Therapy, in effect, involves the translation of emotions into words: You must be able to describe— *from the gut level*—your emotional and attendant physiological feelings. But the overly concrete, withdrawn, lonely child has not yet learned that words can be used to convey feelings. Thus, a program that is successful in teaching communication skills—including nonverbal communication—is as essential for his emotional health as it is for his social development.

EMOTIONAL UNRESPONSIVENESS

Effective and acceptable communication implies a certain degree of emotional response. We are not comfortable with people who seem preoccupied, detached, distant, uninterested. The obligatory smile that is turned on and off too abruptly fools no one. If we are describing some recent pleasant events and we are in a good frame of mind, we expect others to *feel* a little of our happiness. On the other hand, when circumstances are grievable, we expect others to feel—and to demonstrate—some degree of grief. We can never become truly concerned with those who evidence only surface behavior. We demand some depth of feeling, some emotional involvement. In short, we do not care for those who are uncaring.

Many reasons for emotional unresponsiveness exist. There are, of course, those individuals who, though perceptive and intelligent, are too egotistical, manipulative, and selfish to relate to others. Sociopaths (sometimes called psychopaths) may benefit through therapy, but they must choose to be treated and be willing to change. Probably only a small percentage of emotional unresponsiveness can be attributed to sociopathic tendencies.

It is quite possible to have feelings—appropriate, in-depth, and absolutely normal in every respect—but not be able to show them. Kronick (1975, 51) explains the relationship between the learning disabled adolescent's poverty of response and past parental proscription:

> . . . It has been my experience that learning-disabled persons typically feel sorrow and joy as deeply as others; but there are reasons other than the pleasure-pain principle to explain their lack of affect.
>
> In the learning-disabled adolescent's childhood years he exhibited an exaggerated response to stimuli, laughing or crying too loudly, moving his entire body in a plastic infantile response to

excitement, and lashing out in anger and frustration. His parents, being concerned with the inappropriateness of this excessive emotionality, suppressed it. Consequently, part of the adolescent's poverty of response may represent inhibition; his parents may have done too thorough a job . . . [One such youngster] commented, "I'm not sure how to respond to a situation, so I do nothing."

Emotional unresponsiveness is sometimes tied up to depression. Psychologists are becoming aware that depression is not limited to adults. Some children, also, are pervasively unhappy. Their preoccupation with their own problems—whether real or imagined—puts them in an impenetrable "isolation booth." They remain noninvolved (often seemingly bored) with others because the obstacles in their own lives seem insurmountable and inescapable. In rare fleeting moments, when they do attend to others, they see them as successful, happy, and in the mainstream. These glimpses compound their feeling of alienation and create twinges of envy and anger—an anger that flourishes and gradually turns inward in the form of increased depression. They feel nothing matters, so why try—and this includes communicating and empathizing with others. Moreover, this constant display of the "blahs" repels others whose efforts to socialize are rejected. This, of course, promotes loneliness since the prime arena for demonstration of feelings—that is, spontaneous and informal socializing experiences—is rapidly contracting.

In other instances, emotional unresponsiveness may be tied in with the very lessons that we (parents, teachers, close acquaintances) teach them. We tend to teach conformity, especially where the child has evidenced some significant degree of failure—academically, socially, athletically, etc. We want him to be—and to act—like "everybody else." But the feeling and display of emotions, and, in fact, all facets of emotional functioning are, by their very nature, highly personalized and idiosyncratic. If we are too successful in pushing conformity, the individual may develop the *habit* of keeping his feelings to himself in his unsuccessful attempt to "fit in." Kronick (1975, 18) believes that ". . . our efforts towards conformity may have crippled much individuality and that we must find a way of preserving that precious commodity."

Teachers may pursue task analysis and behaviorism too vigorously. This is particularly true in those cases where a learning problem is present and remediation (or prescriptive teaching) is inaugurated: The teacher breaks the terminal task into a hierarchy of subgoals and commences teaching step by step, as she endeavors to impart a specific knowledge or skill. Undisputably, this philosophy of instruction is valuable (even more so when it comes to educating handicapped learners), but it should not be the sole approach. All learning is not linear. Some of it progresses in a "leap" rather than step by step. There is no question that the child must be taught specific, well-defined skills, but he must also be encouraged to explore, to imagine, to create, and *to discover.* The joy of sudden discovery (the "Eureka Phenomenon") is essentially an emotional experience—especially when contrasted with the more sedate (but perhaps equally satisfying) cognitive experience of learning those discrete instructional frames that the teacher teaches. By downgrading exploration and discovery, we may be stifling emotional responsiveness as well.

Finally, we may, by our very example, be reinforcing the surface quality of communication in those we regard as "different." We tend to pamper, placate, to speak in platitudes, to "talk down" to those whom we judge to be impaired, intellectually, socially, or behaviorally. We engage in patter, niceties, and at best, are tolerant—*but never genuinely interested.* We refrain from exposing our feelings to them. This lesson that communication has nothing to do with emotions may "take" too well!

Shallow emotional functioning can be linked with egocentricity. As Kronick (1975, 21) so ably puts it, "If one doesn't regard the world outside oneself as important, one won't respond unduly to what happens in it."

Then, too, lack of emotional response can be seen as a reaction to others' constant rejection. We want to be cherished by those we cherish. But since it is painfully clear that we are *not* valued, we cannot invest too much of ourselves emotionally.

Sometimes, communicating without feeling occurs if a child is withdrawn, bored, has a short attention span, has a sense of unrelatedness with the mainstream, has few interests and hobbies, is not resourceful, is definitely not "well-rounded," and is not goal

70

directed. Here, the child manifests *shallowness, in general,* and emotional shallowness is merely one aspect.

There are direct connections between nonverbal communication lacks and emotional unresponsiveness. Excessive egocentricity and concretism may be present. The child simply has not *learned* to regard communication as a vehicle for expressing feelings. Moreover, insufficient social experiences, the existence of a poor feedback mechanism, plus possible perceptual handicaps make it difficult for him to learn how to *express* nonverbally such feelings as suspicion, injured innocence, cynicism, anger, pleasure, warmth. In other words, a child can *feel* emotions "normally," yet be unable to *express* them in recognizable nonverbal signals. Technically, this is *quasi*-emotional shallowness, but it will, of course, be regarded as the real thing. Besides, if someone misses nuances, doesn't get the gist of social situations, can't fathom others' moods and intentions, then he will not react emotionally—even if he could! Clearly, then, ineffective nonverbal communication—whatever its origin—can result in emotional unresponsiveness.

The converse is also true. Emotional unresponsiveness generates a life-style that is "out of it." This affects the quality of communication, drastically curtailing the number of important, in-depth nonverbal messages transmitted and received. In short, shallow emotion (or the semblance of it) nurtures shallow communication. Thus, the very vehicle (that is, frequent and sustained experience in emotional communication) by which emotionally unresponsive persons could become more proficient in nonverbal communication of emotions is denied them. Shallow emotions and meager social perception may not be synonymous, but at the very least they have a strong kinship.

REFERENCES

Connolly, Christopher. "Social and Emotional Factors in Learning Disabilities." In Helmer Myklebust, ed. *Progress in Learning Disabilities,* vol. 2. New York: Grune and Stratton, 1971, pp. 151–178.

Kronick, Doreen. *What About Me? The Learning Disabled Adolescent.* San Rafael, Calif.: Academic Therapy Publications, 1975.

McCandless, Boyd. *Children: Behavior and Development.* 2nd ed. New York: Holt, Rinehart, and Winston, 1967.

Ross, Alan O. *Psychological Aspects of Learning Disabilities and Reading Disorders.* New York: McGraw-Hill, 1976.

Sarason, Seymour, *et al. Anxiety in Elementary School Children.* New York: Wiley, 1960.

Tannenbaum, P. "Initial Attitude Toward Source and Concept as Factors in Attitude Change Through Communication." *Public Opinion Quarterly,* 20 (1956): 413–425.

CHAPTER 6

Perceptual Difficulties

Jimmy is ten years old. His teacher complains that he frequently dawdles instead of getting started. He doesn't respond as expected to such messages as "now," "later," "in just a few moments," etc. At times he talks too quickly—and at other times, too slowly. He frequently bolts his food. His mother has noted other odd behaviors such as hanging up the telephone and then saying "Goodbye."

Henrietta is in the third grade. When the school guidance counselor asked the teacher what was it about Henrietta that made her so unpopular, the teacher pointed out that she talked too loudly, using the same voice volume whether the listener was near her or far from her. Also she frequently stands too close to people when she speaks to them.

Two of Frank's tenth-grade classmates are talking about him. "He sure is odd," says the first. "Sometimes he practically crushes your fingers when he shakes hands with you, and at other times his handshake is as limp as a fish." The other assents, then adds, "And he does such strange things. The other day, I asked him a question and he moved his hands in a funny way. After a while, I realized that he didn't know the answer and was trying to shrug his shoulders, but, you know what? He was actually shrugging his elbows!"

Bobby recently joined the Boy Scouts, but he doesn't make friends there any more easily than he does in his fifth-grade class. A closer inspection would reveal that, when others are talking, he frequently interrupts them. When this occurs, they frown, register quizzical expressions, shake their heads disapprovingly, and sometimes even begin whispering about him. All of these responses seem to go unnoticed. He goes right along, interrupting as usual.

Each of the above illustrates some specific aspect of perceptual disorder. Jimmy was unable to judge time intervals. Henrietta had a poorly developed sense of space. Frank could not readily interpret signals from his own body regarding movement and muscle tone. The many messages that his friends were sending could not easily be assimilated by Bobby and hence did not help him modify his behavior.

Obviously perceptual impairment can contribute directly to a child's inability to receive nonverbal communication signals. Children who have difficulty differentiating circles from ovals, *h*'s from *n*'s, the words *saw* and *was,* and in remembering the sequence of letters in a word they have just seen often have difficulty distinguishing a frown from a smile, recognizing a raised eyebrow when they see it, understanding a nonverbal sequence "unit" (for example, an upward gaze indicating consideration followed by pursed lips denoting doubt followed by slight shaking of the head indicating rejection). Likewise, the child who hears "hop-si-tal" for *hospital,* can't distinguish between *bad* and *bed,* and can't hear the difference between a higher and lower musical note may encounter similar problems in identifying a sarcastic tone, differentiating between an excited and a calm voice, hearing a sigh of relief as distinct from a sigh of boredom, and in recognizing whether or not a given "oh, yeah" is defiant, accepting, conveying "I just remembered," or is merely being used to confirm an inner thought of the speaker.

Certainly spatial orientation problems can result in errors in interpreting social and personal space cues of the speaker: The message that "I am sharing a secret with you" is missed by the child who doesn't perceive that the speaker is standing unusually close to him. Similarly, temporal distortion can cause an individual to stare at a person for an inordinately long time instead of proferring the acceptable casual glance. Figure-ground confusion can contribute to inattentiveness. Moreover, a child who concentrates on minor details will often miss the point of many social situations. Impaired peripheral perception, coupled with egocentricity—"*I* am talking to (at?) person A now, so I can't possibly acknowledge person B at the same time"—could result in the virtual snubbing of a third party during a conversation.

Some children are unable to cope with multiple sensory stimuli. In school, this can be seen in the child who closes his eyes "to hear better" and in pupils who excel in silent reading but perform poorly when reading aloud when they must simultaneously use their ears, eyes, and voice. Such "overload-prone" children are likely to suffer in spontaneous social situations as well since these are relatively unstructured and no one regulates the flow of sensory stimuli.

Just as visual-motor incoordination can account for an inability to copy correctly from the blackboard, it may also result in imprecise hand gestures. In other words, a child with visual-motor deficits may correctly perceive the manner in which others produce gestures (for example, beckoning "come here" with the crooked index finger, signaling "stop" with an upraised hand, waving "go away"), but he cannot readily duplicate them. In the same way, an impaired body image may result in body language that is misleading, not easily recognizable, "different."

AVENUES OF LEARNING

If you say that a given child has perceptual impairments, you are immediately asked, "Is it visual perception?" "Auditory perception?" "Both?" "Is it a tactile problem or a kinesthetic deficit?" (The senses of taste and smell are not nearly so important educationally.) It is not surprising that most diagnostic procedures seek to identify which functions are impaired and which are intact. Such information can shed light on the way the individual processes information (his so-called learning style) and it also suggests how the impaired functions can be compensated for by working through

75

the intact area, or using a multisensory approach in which the strong sense "carries" and leads the weak one.

THE "ALL OR NOTHING" ASPECT OF PERCEPTION

It would be most unusual for a child to say: "That man has a suit like Father's. He walks like Father. He has glasses and a moustache like Father. It *is* Father!" Most likely, he would recognize him all at once. That is, it is not only the individual details, themselves, but also the *interrelationship* of these parts as well as the *context* in which they appear, which define the gist of a situation. For example, haven't we all had the experience of looking at a cartoon and not understanding it? We see all the details, we read the legend correctly, yet we literally miss the point. Similarly, you can miss the point of a social transaction if you don't grasp the interrelationship of various nonverbal signals or the context in which they occur. And it goes without saying that the essence of a social situation will not be divined if you have difficulty in receiving body language cues (for example, you may not notice a nod, may not see the difference between a mouth that is agape and one that is only slightly open, may not be able readily to feel the difference between a weak handshake and a firm one, may not realize that you are standing too close to the person with whom you are speaking).

Each of us has a very real need to systematize, to arrange, to order, to understand our environment. If an ambiguous shape (e.g., ⋈) is presented, we are apt to report seeing an hourglass —or a bow tie standing on edge—or two links of a bracelet. If incomplete data is presented, we generally fill in the missing pieces —and often automatically without actually realizing that we have done so. Hence ☐ is perceived as a box, ⋯⋮ is seen as a T, and the slurring of "gov-ment" is heard as "government."

Young children need more sensory data than older children in order to derive meaning from incomplete stimuli. Similarly, neurologically impaired individuals need more "pieces" of the whole than do the neurologically intact. Ross (1954, 566–572) examined brain-injured army patients in tasks including ability to

76

recognize (by feeling) thumbtack patterns of letters, numbers, and well-known symbols in various stages of completeness: the complete outline; a few tacks omitted; least number of tacks that could be used and still preserve the essence of the original pattern. It was found that the brain-injured subjects required a greater degree of completeness of form outline than did the control group (normals) to recognize the pattern.

This, of course, has implication for any training program designed to increase social perception among those with perceptual deficits: At first, the nonverbal communication cues should be exaggerated and relatively numerous. Gradually, fewer cues should be used and introduced more subtly.

PERCEPTION AND INSIGHT

There is one definitional aspect of perception that is usually ignored by authors who write primarily of learning disabilities, perceptual disorders, neurological impairments, and the like. It is that facet of perception that denotes insight and intuition. If an individual is able to grasp the true intentions of others, if he is unusually adept in picking up subtle, *almost imperceptible* nonverbal cues, if he can read between the lines, if he has a real knack for sensing others' moods and feelings despite their efforts to keep them hidden, don't we pronounce him intuitive, insightful, *perceptive?* The traditional connotation of perception is relatively simple since it deals only with the *initial* meaning we attach to raw sensory data (sounds, sights, sensations of touch, awareness of body position). But the other is more advanced since it is cognitive in nature and smacks of reasoning, conceptualization, "putting two and two together." This insightful aspect of perception can probably be viewed as a summation of all the individual components of social perception. To put it differently, if we can succeed in teaching a socially imperceptive child how to derive optimal meaning from facial expression, gesture, eye movement, body movement, vocal inflection, the space the speaker allows to stand between himself and the listener, then he will have the prerequisites for the development of this highest level of perception. The emergence of insight, in turn, signifies—or can effect—a diminishing of gullibility, a reduction of illogical conclusions and responses, a lessening of anxiety, more appropriate attention behavior, a more effective communication style, and, ultimately, a more favorable self-concept.

REFERENCE

Ross, Alan O. "Tactual Perception of Form by the Brain-Injured." *Journal of Abnormal and Social Psychology* 49 (October 1954): 566–572.

PART 3

Toward Diminishing Loneliness

Parents who, over a period of years, have witnessed and empathized with the pains of rejection suffered by their children may become overprotective. It is patently easier and less threatening to refrain from attempting something new than to experience once again that dreaded ostracism. Perhaps they won't send Billy to nursery school, or to sleep-away camp, or allow him to join the Boy Scouts. Even an invitation to sleep over at a friend's house evokes visions of a crying child phoning his parents to "take me home, Johnny doesn't want me here anymore." As Billy grows into adolescence and young adulthood, worries over how he will handle encounters with strangers when traveling on his own, or how he can possibly drive a car, come to the fore. Growing independence seems to pose ever-increasing threats to his physical and psychological well-being.

The fear is not unnatural, but acting on it can only retard the wished for diminution of loneliness. Parents must accept the idea that gradually they will have to "let go" in order to use the guides set forth in the next chapters most productively.

In this vein, a special word to teachers is pertinent. They must be aware that although the lonely child needs training in social perception, the child's sensitivity must be a paramount consideration at all times.

Although stressing socialization, we recognize that socially imperceptive children are not at all expert in productive use of "spare" time. (In the case of lonely children, spare time is often overabundant and, in fact, may include a major portion of their waking hours.) This, then, requires teaching in solitary diversions. Introduction by parents or teachers to games of solitaire, needlework skills, crossword puzzles, gardening, music appreciation, woodworking, arts and crafts, or any hobbies like coin or stamp collecting can keep time spent alone from being so onerous as to become a source of deep depression.

It is not just happenstance that the chapters giving advice on socialization in this part include both teachers and parents. It is the authors' belief that the richest harvest is reaped when parents and teachers work together for the child who is their concern.

CHAPTER 7

The Parent's Role

HELPING THE VERY YOUNG CHILD
TO SOCIALIZE

You, the parents, will most likely be the ones to embark on a program designed to diminish loneliness in your child. Probably you will be the first to perceive that your child is lonely.

Oddly, among very young children, often as young as three and four years of age, it is frequently his age peers who first diagnose the "differentness" that makes a given youngster a candidate for rejection. If you observe carefully, you will discover certain symptoms (the child is never sought out, or is pushed away from the group) that require intervention. The purpose of this intervention is to prevent patterns of rejection from becoming set and thus much more difficult to correct.

Children begin social interaction via parallel play. That is, they enjoy and want to be close to others of their own age, but they are not yet ready to share and play together. They sit, perhaps both in the same sandbox, each with his own pail and shovel and each doing his "own thing" and apparently paying no attention to the other. They may even be talking but no dialogue is taking place. They talk *about* what they are doing: "I put sand in my pail and

83

make a big house." No response is given nor is one expected. The verbalizations are not made for socializing; rather, they are a way for the child to organize, to label, to structure what he is doing.

This parallel play is not always calm and peaceful. There are times when Betty's pail or other equipment suddenly looks much more attractive to Jimmy than his own. Jimmy grabs. Betty screams or hits. And a small riot ensues. This kind of melee is quite normal but unnerving for parents. Expect it and be prepared to calm ruffled feelings. Don't become involved simply because your child is the victim. Actually, a more valid reason for concern is when it is your child who is always the grabber or the one to display more aggressive and destructive behavior (using his shovel to hammer on his companion's head, destroying the products of the other child's efforts).

If behavior of this kind is observed, it is best to remove the child at once from the setting and engage in some other quiet activity with him. Make notes (mental, or better yet written) of how long the children were together before the problem arose. Plan then to shorten the next period of social play. Your child may not yet be ready for a more extended interval. Shorten the time to the period during which the children demonstrated that they could play together peacefully. Gradually the blocks of time can be increased. Your child may simply require a fifteen-minute break, and then play can be resumed.

HYPERACTIVITY AND AGGRESSIVENESS AS CAUSES OF LONELINESS

If you are faced with a more acute problem (and this can be the case with a very distractible, hyperactive child) wherein your offspring really is incapable of even five minutes of parallel play, you will have to become an integral part of the group. You'll have to be right in the setting, *guiding* your child's play while the other child is there. This, then, becomes a more structured, protective period and still a form of parallel play is taking place. Make attempts, as time goes on, to leave or to shift your position for a few minutes at a time to test whether or not your child has built any more tolerance for the more normal setting. Remember that the youngster who is companion to this child will not accept abuse—nor should he. Moreover, even if *he* should be willing to do so, *his parents* will soon find excuses to keep him away from your youngster, and, in this manner, take the first step in creating a lonely child.

INAPPROPRIATE SPEECH AS A CAUSE OF LONELINESS

It is not only in aggressive behavior that problems can arise. Some lonely children are not now, nor ever were in any way, aggressive children. Yet somehow they are perceived as "different" and rejected anyway. Perhaps delayed or inappropriate speech and communication is a factor. The child of four or five who cannot verbalize well enough to play the "pretend" games in which the other children engage will not be invited to play. He doesn't know what to say if he is the "cowboy" or the "Indian." If speech itself is lacking or significantly more infantile than that of other children his age, professional help may be needed. At the very least, his speech should be evaluated. Many colleges, some children's hospitals, and clinics have such services available. You yourself can do certain things to help. Talk to your child, read to him, and especially *listen* to him. Require spoken language and do not accept gestures when he wants something. *Do* accept approximations of the correct word or words. Reward effort and slowly raise the level of expectation. "Wahwah" for *water* instead of pointing to the faucet is a good beginning, but work toward a clear "water" and even an "I want water" as time goes by.

Some children, despite an adequate ability to verbalize and to speak with clarity, may still require special help simply because they talk too much. This is not likely to occur in *very* young children. However, by the age of six or seven, it might become a real problem. For this kind of behavior, the parent will have to help the child limit his verbalizations by giving him direct cues in various social situations. If he is monopolizing a group conversation, the parent must state firmly, "We like to hear what you have

85

to say and we want to hear others, too. Now, it is time for you and me to listen while Mary talks to us." A very good time to promote proper amounts as well as appropriate conversational offerings is during a game period shared by parents and children. Conversation about the game can be encouraged with smiles and nods and phrases like, "I'm glad you are enjoying this new game," "The things you are saying about this game show you have learned it well."

A LONELY CHILD OR A "LONER"?

It is expected that children by the age of four (sometimes even younger) will be able to play in another child's home, at a local playground, or just "outside" the house in suburban settings without direct adult supervision. If your child is not able to do this easily, then you must begin making careful observations and note exactly what is happening. Does your child "reach out" toward the other children and try to become part of their group? Is he merely tolerated and allowed to remain on the periphery or, even worse, scorned and told to "go away"? If he does go to visit a neighboring child, is he welcomed? Does he remain with his companion for a suitable length of time? Do any of the children's mothers complain about his aggressiveness or "pestiness"? Are they, in fact, not pleased to have him around?

The answers to these questions can indicate a definite pattern. But look further. Is your child really rejected? There is a possibility that he is not. If other children frequently seek him out and he is reluctant to join them, your child is not a "lonely" child. Rather, he is one who *chooses* to remain alone. This type of child—often bright and creative—is happiest playing with one "selected" companion or in his own company. You can tell the difference by judging how well your child does when he is in a peer setting (for instance, a birthday party, or on the infrequent occasions when he does decide to participate in a larger group activity). If you see that he enjoys the group and that the group welcomes him, he is probably a child who has his own style of socialization that is effective and normal for him.

On the other hand, if everything you observe leads to the conclusion that your youngster is indeed not wanted, not happy, and alone only because he has no other option, it is time to step in and begin a program of remediation.

TEACHING THE LONELY CHILD HOW TO PLAY

Children need to play with other children. And they learn how to play well together through frequent experiences and because their social perception reinforces those behaviors that are acceptable and decreases the occurrence of those their peers won't tolerate. The lonely child is the one whose perceptions are faulty and who does not correctly read the feedback obtainable from his playmates. He does not readily recognize when they are pleased with him and when they do not like his actions. Even when verbally told in no uncertain terms that a specific behavior is disliked, he may not be able to control that behavior because he possesses some of the traits and disorders discussed in Part 2 of this book. This child requires preparation and instruction in socializing with his peers. His parents are probably best able to provide the initial remediation.

First, the child needs play experience. If he is not getting enough of it outside the family, then the family must provide these experiences for him. Moms and dads can certainly engage the lonely child (and his siblings too!) in some of the games children usually learn from each other. These include card games (Go Fish, Spit, Old Maid), board games (Monopoly, Checkers), and ball games (Monkey in the Middle, Catch, Marbles, Tag) and many others. Since his age peers are probably adept at these games, the lonely child is further handicapped if he does not know them. It is wise to observe the games in which the neighborhood children indulge as a basis for his "curriculum." Help the child learn to lose gracefully too. Praise for improvement and good sportsmanship is more important than social rewards for winning. If, for some reason, you are not able to play with your child, then an alternative might be considered. High school youngsters are often looking for part-time jobs, and a bright, warm youngster could be hired to be a surrogate "social teacher."

PROVIDING COMPANIONS FOR
THE LONELY CHILD

While making sure that the child gets experience at games is essential, it is even more important to provide him with the company of children his own age. At the beginning, he may not be capable of "playing" with them. Your job then is twofold. First, make certain that those children chosen as companions find the experience an enjoyable one. Unsatisfactory experiences can use up the supply of willing companions very quickly! Second, plan and structure the social experiences so that they build in two ways: (1) toward independent play, and (2) toward suitable time blocks.

To begin, a neighboring child or a classmate might be invited to listen to a story and have a milk and cookies snack. Be sure the time is limited, probably no more than fifteen minutes at first. Don't be lulled into believing that because the playmate seems to enjoy the time so much, he'd probably like to stay a while longer and watch TV or play a new game. Remember, the most successful performers are those who have learned to leave while the audience still wants more—that's the way they keep them coming back. The parent is just as anxious to have the playmate return and facilitate more social experience. As with the very young child, these encounters require a large degree of parental structure in planning the activities, setting the time limit and, *ever so slowly,* increasing the degree of independence, and lengthening time periods. The initial burden on the parents is indeed a heavy one, but the rewards (especially in the child's social future) are so great that they are truly worthwhile.

ALLEVIATING LONELINESS IN
THE OLDER CHILD

Do not assume that if your child is older—ten or eleven or even teen-aged—that a parentally guided pattern of remediation cannot be started. It can be done with certain modifications. Older children are not so easily lured into joining your lonely child for a game of Checkers or Monopoly. These are pretty "old hat" to them and hold no special appeal. On the other hand, an outing (which must also be structured and planned in advance) may be just the ticket. Choose something wherein the "friend" and your child are not likely to ignore one another completely. Therefore a movie, or ballet, or a baseball game are not the first choices. Both children can too easily become mere spectators with almost no interaction. A miniature golf game, bowling, a visit to the zoo, the beach, or a playland are better choices. Keep the time blocks well-structured. Plan a short meal and guide the conversation so that both children are involved and do more talking than you do. From this initial stage (always keeping time dosages in mind), a short quiet game period in your home can be introduced. It might be politic to teach both children a "new" game or to have on hand one that is a current favorite or fad.

If, as time goes by, the social experiences between the two children seem pleasant, then a third child might be introduced into the group. Don't hesitate to drop this if a threesome proves to be more than your child can handle.

FINDING A COMPANION FOR
THE OLDER CHILD

Sometimes a pattern of rejection toward your child has become so established among the neighborhood children that none will agree to be his companion. In that case, his teacher may be a source of help. There may be at least one student in his class who seems drawn to him, or another who seems equally lonely. If that is so, you could ask the teacher to help you contact this child's parents and proceed with the previously described strategies for increasing socialization skills.

The authors have, on occasion, advised parents to move to a new neighborhood if all the avenues toward companionship seem closed. This does indeed seem a drastic remedy, but we must recognize that the "illness" of loneliness is a very serious one.

89

SUGGESTIONS FOR ALLEVIATING LONELINESS IN THE ADOLESCENT AND YOUNG ADULT

It is not infrequent that parents first recognize the symptoms of loneliness in their children only when they reach late adolescence and young adulthood. This is understandable since, during the early years, such experiences as nursery schools, elementary and upper level schools, homework, TV, and family outings accounted for a vast majority of the child's time. Now, perhaps, schooling is over, jobs are either not available or are too easily lost, and the parents' friends are no longer taking their children out with them. Now, suddenly the sad picture of a lonely young person becomes dramatically apparent. And the parents may berate themselves (unjustly, in most cases) for past errors of omission and wonder if there is anything at all they can do.

Nurturing Interests that Have a High Social Index

There are several helpful courses open. First, try to get the young person involved in some kind of sport, hobby, or interest that requires the participation of other people. Stamp collecting may well be a productive hobby, but it is not likely to promote socialization. Tennis, bowling, bridge, politics can lead to more social contact. This is especially true if encouragement toward *organizations* such as bowling leagues, bridge or political clubs is forthcoming. You may at first have to become a part of these groups until such time as the young person finds a comfortable niche. While it is true that, in general, one must lead the individual toward ever-increasing numbers of social contacts and experiences, great care must be taken to make success likely. In short, you will be performing a disservice to the lonely young person if all you offer is more opportunities for failure.

Arranging Friendships

In years gone by, parents found mates for—and arranged—the marriages of their children. This old tradition can be brought up-to-date in our efforts to diminish loneliness in young people. We should not limit these arrangements to marriages, but include friendships as well. If you, the parent, keep tuned in to the stories that friends and acquaintances tell of their own children and the social problems they have, you may very likely learn of another lonely young person eager for companionship. It is absolutely true that there is a vast difference between having only one friend to share things with and having no one at all.

Expanding One's Social Options

Any step that can, in some way, expand social options should be considered and undertaken. Learning to drive immediately increases a person's social periphery and could even make it possible to join a more accepting social group in another town or to visit with a friend who lives a distance away. It can increase the number of employment alternatives, hence providing additional social opportunities.

Involvement with volunteer groups expands the lonely person's range of social activities and can contribute toward making him more interesting. The more areas in which he becomes involved, the more he is able to capture the attention and concern of other people. Being needed and fulfilling another's needs go a long way toward building self-esteem. The church or synagogue can be a source of friendly contacts. Religious or purely social groups abound and active members are usually welcomed. A visit to your priest, minister, or rabbi might pave the way for a warm welcome to the lonely young person.

COUNSELING FOR PARENTS

You as a parent have an especially difficult job in your efforts to guide your child toward pleasant and meaningful social experiences. This is particularly true because you are emotionally involved in the process. Wanting the best for your child, you may see only the worst; witnessing the pain inflicted on your child, you may suffer a worse pain. Nonetheless, it is important that you separate your needs from those of your lonely child. Counsel from a professional therapist can make you less vulnerable and more effective.

CHAPTER 8
The Teacher's Role

RECOGNIZING THE LONELY CHILD AS A PSYCHOLOGICAL PROBLEM

Psychologists are finally beginning to regard the lonely child as a matter for serious concern. Flaste (1977, B4) notes that such children seem always to be on the periphery of social activity and are so little noticed that their peers do not even mention them in lists of *least*-liked companions. Psychologists record that these children never seem to know what to do or to say in play situations. The one positive note sounded by professionals is that these "hovering" children can be coached in the art of being sociable. Skills taught these youngsters include: eye contact, initiation of games, continuation of the games once they have begun, cooperation, sharing, and just being pleasant. While some parents can be effective in coaching these skills, others may tend to be punitive and then perhaps teachers may prove more successful. Certainly, teachers feel obliged to offer help to those pupils who encounter academic difficulties. The ostracized child is failing in "friends" and needs the teacher's intervention even more than does the child reading below grade level.

FIRST STEPS IN HELPING THE
LONELY CHILD

The preceding chapter mentions the many ways that parents can help their lonely child become more social. If all these strategies were followed, the teacher's role would be minimal. Unfortunately, many lonely children come from families who have no idea what to do about the problem. This lack, then, points to the first step for the teacher of any lonely child: Arrange a parent-teacher conference. If the parent is asked the right questions by the teacher, he or she may find it easier to recognize—and talk about—the problem. Parents, often on the defensive, may quickly answer in the affirmative if asked, "Does Jimmy have many friends?" Further, gentle probing will be necessary. "Are his friends often somewhat younger than he?" "Do you approve of the friends Jimmy plays with?" "Do Jimmy's friends call for him often?" "What kind of games do they play?" "How much of the time is Jimmy alone, watching TV or playing by himself?" "Is he invited to many parties?" This kind of questioning may lead a parent who, subconsciously, has been denying the problem or who has feelings of guilt, to see her child's social deficits more clearly. The teacher must, of course, be understanding and in no way accusatory. At this point, if the parent shows an interest in improving the situation, the teacher can make some of the suggestions mentioned in chapter seven.

Sometimes the parent shows no interest, continues a pattern of denial, or seems totally incapable of following a suitable course of remedial action. The child's problem is not lessened nor is the teacher's responsibility in any way diminished. The problem is, in fact, magnified and now the teacher's role is even more important as well as more difficult.

HELP FOR THE LONELY CHILD IN
THE EARLY GRADES

Teachers of very young children (nursery through second grade) are in an excellent position to help an ostracized child. He is young enough so that serious overlays of emotional disturbance and patterns of rejection and withdrawal have probably not yet been set.

Young children are very prone to reflect a teacher's attitude toward their peers. If the teacher accepts and shows approval and liking for a child, even one who demonstrates inappropriate speech or behavior at times, the classmates will probably also like that child. (It must be stressed that the effective—and affective—teacher always accepts the person of the child, though she will not approve of offensive actions, verbal or physical.)

New York City's Curriculum Bulletin for *Oral Communication, Grades K–6* (1976–1977, 1) describes the kind of classroom setting in which children's communication (and social) skills can emerge and flourish. The atmosphere should be relaxed and free of distractions and the teacher's verbalizations must be carefully planned. Pupils' responses to questions should not be repeated nor should their individual names precede an inquiry from the teacher. The children will be too easily tempted then to tune one another out and listen only to the words of the teacher. This would serve to lessen the much-needed interaction among the pupils themselves. Children should be encouraged to speak in a "classroom" voice—not as loud as an outdoor shout but loud enough for peers to hear with ease. When a shy quiet child does speak too softly, the teacher should not fall into the trap of repeating what is said or tell the child, "We can't hear what you have to say." Because she is aware of which child is likely to answer in this manner, the teacher should try to place herself close enough for her to hear the child's words. Then she is in a position to say something like, "That was a very good answer [or idea] you had, Karen. Would you repeat it in a real classroom voice so your classmates can share it?" At this point, helping the child to rise from her seat and warmly embracing her might give her the impetus to follow the verbal suggestion more easily.

Teaching Communication Skills

The teacher of the young child should realize that communication skills are needed to help him feel good about himself, to increase his desire to share, to think and learn, and to enable the teacher to understand the youngster's inner being. Therefore, she should plan as carefully for lessons in communications as she does for any other subject. Most teachers feel that they are not adequately trained to do "speech therapy." Specialized training would be fine, but currently there is so much excellent material available to teach communications skills (see Appendix) that she may well find it easier than teaching simple addition. An important reason for this is that the teaching of communications requires the active participation of the children themselves.

Many of the activities found in this book and in various other texts, kits, and programs listed in the Appendix are intrinsically motivating because they are fun. It would be a good idea for a teacher embarking on a program of communications improvement to read one of the simple and informative texts in this field written for teachers (see *Texts* recommended in the Appendix).

Classroom Atmosphere

The general atmosphere of the classroom and, of course, the demeanor of the teacher must be warm and sufficiently accepting to nurture socialization. Cedoline (1977, 13) has some special words in this vein: "Greet each child; occasionally eat with the class; provide moments of humor; tell the children you love them; . . . hug them all . . ." A classroom that is not frighteningly overpermissive (and usually then chaotic) nor overly authoritarian can be achieved when the teacher is actively consistent in praise as well as punishment. If such a setting is the kind in which children spend their school hours, they are not so likely to be punitive toward the child who has a hard time socializing. However, since this kind of milieu is not often found outside a friendly structured classroom, the young, nonsocially adept child must be given much support and frequent opportunities to be a friend or companion.

Specific Suggestions for Promoting Socialization

It is a good idea to make the child pleasantly visible to his classmates. If he is a withdrawn youngster and he is given the job of distributing "nice things" like crayons, snacktime milk and cookies, or of putting commendation checks on the "Classroom Behavior Chart" he will be seen in a more positive light. Even if the lonely or ostracized child is one who exhibits occasional aggressive behavior, these monitorships will show him in a better and more appealing role.

When any tasks are to be performed that can be done as well by two, the teacher should choose the lonely child and a classmate she knows to be of a kind, even temperament. Game rules should be arranged so that this child is not always last to be chosen or perhaps not even selected at all. This can be done by narrowing the options: "Today when we're playing Ducks and Geese, we'll pick all the boys who are sitting near the windows first" (and, of course, Jimmy is near the window) or "We'll pick boys with brown eyes first today."

Often, even academic work can be done in partnership. Sometimes it is not so important to see whether or not the child can get one hundred percent on his assigned reading workbook page as it is to see the child working, conversing, and cooperating with another child assigned the same page.

Even in a highly individualized curriculum there are occasions —and these should be capitalized on—when a small group or just two children can work together. Buddy tests in spelling, social studies reports, arts and crafts—all offer ample opportunity for social interaction within the classroom.

If it is the classroom teacher's policy to send the children on errands or even to the bathroom in pairs, then pairing the lonely child fairly often and with different partners is advised. It may be possible then to find a particular child with whom he can get along well.

Show-and-Tell time is a period when the young lonely child can function well if the teacher arranges for special help and provides encouragement. She may want to contact the parents so they can help the child find some "thing" to talk about. (Initially *things* are easier to talk about than *events*.) Perhaps a regular routine can be set up whereby some special activity or object can be focused on during the weekend and shared in class on Mondays. A little coaching might be in order and the teacher can tell the mother how this might best be achieved.

Since, in the early grades, a good portion of time is devoted to playtime learning, the teacher has frequent opportunity to observe and hopefully to do some charting to see how much the child is improving socially. The astute teacher will note any increases in conversations initiated by the child or in approaches to the child by other pupils. She can stimulate this by using the lonely child as an intermediary: "Will you please tell Jane that I'm ready to check her spelling homework?" or "Mary will need a green crayon for this, will you get one for her?" Probably the most important concept for the teachers of younger children to understand is that they are in position to promote those classroom experiences that can prevent the socially inept child from becoming locked into a rigid block of social failure and loneliness. Liking, supporting, teaching, carefully observing, providing appropriate opportunities and a socially conducive setting may make a turnaround possible before this child becomes an ostracized, hovering nonperson.

IMPROVING SOCIALIZATION IN INTERMEDIATE GRADES

Lonely children in the intermediate elementary school grades can benefit from almost all the suggestions made in the first section of this chapter. In deference to their more mature status, certain slight changes are in order and several additional ideas can be used.

Integrating Social Skills with Gym

Some rather simple strategies for choosing game players were mentioned on page 96. When similar games are played by older children, the same methods may be used. However, they will not go over well with boys and girls ready for team games—like punchball, kickball, or softball. All youngsters of this age are notorious for spending more time choosing up sides and arguing about who is "first up" than they do in playing. It might be a fruitful idea in many ways to discuss with the class the effectiveness of evenly matched sides as making for a more enjoyable game (more chances to be up, less chance of always winning or losing, and so forth). After enough time has gone by for the children to have evaluated the athletic skills of their peers, permanent teams can be formed. The teacher will ask the children to name the best players (in descending order) and assign them to teams as follows:

Team A	Team B
#1	#2
#4	#3
#5	#6
#8	#7
etc.	

This should make for very even teams. The ostracized child, if he happens to be judged one of the worst players, might find this choosing a rather painful experience—but it need only occur once during the year. In addition, a procedure like the one described above will relieve the lonely child of the terrible burden of having to stand, waiting and waiting (usually to the bitter end) to be chosen for a team each time the class has a gym period.

The teacher may find it desirable to set up three sets of teams—all boys, all girls, and mixed. Often, children of this age like mixed teams, but on occasion they prefer to play a game with members of their own sex.

Using Board and Card Games

At this age, children are ready to play many board and card games. Ordinarily they learn these from each other on those cold or rainy days when outdoor play is not feasible. It goes without saying that the ostracized child who is not playing with his peers is not learning from them. (Of course, the television generation seems to do less of this than their parents and grandparents did. The teacher who introduces these games to her classes may be doing *all* the children a very good turn by offering them an alternative to a steady diet of TV.)

If a socialization program using card and board games is to succeed, it is necessary to set aside a regular time for "social games." The hour before dismissal one day a week (perhaps Thursday or Friday) is probably the best choice. Rules and regulations for this period should be set, understood, and agreed to. Rules should include decisions regarding (1) voice levels, (2) number of different games played, (3) sportsmanship, and (4) choosing games to play.

Children should recognize that board and card games are quiet games and require that their voices be kept modulated. If a child breaks this rule, he should be gently warned and reminded that this infraction necessitates a five-minute time-out from playing should he forget again. If a time-out becomes necessary, a kitchen timer is useful because it enables the child to see the time passing and allows the teacher to concentrate on other things. Consistent, dispassionate use of this behavior-modification technique will probably succeed in keeping the social games period a quiet and peaceful one. This particular rule and its enforcement is especially important for the ostracized child who often has difficulty learning and using the correct voice levels for different places and activities.

Two different games per period should be the limit allowed to any given child. This will prevent the bustle of constant movement to change and begin new games. It will also encourage the youngsters to complete games—a trait to which skilled social interacters respond positively.

Behavior modification can be used to reinforce sportsmanship over competitiveness. Commendations or small rewards given for following the rules, cleanup assistance, and generally cooperative behavior can be very motivating.

Although certain games may be favored by the children during any given period, these favorites tend to change over a span of time. To make choosing easier and fairer, the children should know that anyone who desires to play a particular game and does not get the chance one week, will have his name listed for first choice of that game the next week. If arguments arise over choosing games, "I got it first" or "I want to play too," it is best to let the children solve the disagreements among themselves as often as possible. Insistence that the problem be quietly and amicably resolved within five minutes (another use for the kitchen timer) or all the children in the dispute will take a ten-minute "time-out" from game playing may bring on the solution surprisingly quickly. Moreover, this approach nurtures group communication, mutual decision making, and the ability to compromise productively. Possible alternatives and options should initially be offered by the teacher: one pair playing at first and the odd man playing the winner (for short games); switching at half time; odd man having his name put on a special list for next week.

Before the teacher embarks on a program to provide social games experience, several obstacles may arise that must be considered, and ways to overcome them need to be formulated. The teacher must be prepared to explain, and give cogent arguments, to the administration and to the parents why the time to be used is educational, both socially and academically. Educational aspects of a games program include reading (rules, consequence cards), math (counting moves or money), directionality (as in Checkers, Chess, and Connect Four), vocabulary (Password, Scrabble), long-term memory (card games like Rummy or Casino). In addition, games nurture attention skills, cognitive skills (for example, rules and objectives of a game), and can serve to diminish impulsivity since each player must wait his turn. Most games involve several aspects of academic reinforcement.

Once the teacher has successfully convinced the parents (perhaps via a mimeographed letter) and the administration that the plan for a social period is a valid one, she can request their aid in obtaining games. Many children have games they have tired of or that have parts missing. Missing parts can frequently be obtained inexpensively or free if the teacher writes a request to the manufacturing company. A portion of the funds earmarked for school supplies can sometimes be used to purchase new games. The teacher will probably be willing to use some of her own money to buy some of the less expensive games like playing cards, checkerboards and checkers. Flea markets and garage sales are an excellent source of secondhand, very inexpensive games.

It must be understood that for this to be a real learning experience (especially for the lonely child) the teacher—or classmates—should at times be teaching and learning *new* games. The classroom teacher must know the rules of all the games that the children play. She also needs to be ready to sit with the lonely child (and at least one other child) to play this new game with him.

These suggestions offered for regular track teachers can be used equally well by teachers of special classes for learning disabled or emotionally handicapped children. Even a resource-room teacher or an itinerant teacher can set aside a period during which a group of the children she works with can meet for a games period. The classroom teacher's reports and observations will help the resource person identify the students needing this kind of training.

For the lonely child, the games period *must* be a pleasant one and should also be a source of learning that can be carried with him to his home environment.

Integrating Social Skills with Academic Subjects

In the middle grades, the teacher can find even more opportunity for pairing or grouping in academic subjects. Social studies reports, science experiments, murals, bulletin boards, math and reading reinforcement games, peer tutoring, or just two children working together on the same assignment are all ways to get the lonely child productively involved with others. For the socially inept youngster, pairing is almost certainly better at first. Perhaps some children will not be ready for a group situation because as soon as there are three individuals involved, two can very easily ignore the third. The lonely child would be back on the periphery. Social opportunities within the academic sphere must be planned carefully. They need structure and rules similar to those previously cited for participation in social games. The lonely child should be considered, but never to the point of being singled out. For example, he should not always be paired when the rest of the class is not. All of the suggestions made for children working together can make for a pleasanter, easier (albeit structured) atmosphere in which all children can learn.

Communication Skills

We strongly urge that the suggestions made here, as well as in other books, kits, and programs listed in the Appendix, be investigated and tried. All of those recommended are quite simple to learn and extremely easy to integrate into the class curriculum. Many have been used or have been observed in use by the authors and have succeeded well in their stated aims.

Older children are most interested in and capable of participating in role playing, mime, puppetry, charades, and even skits. Many of the professionally made games involving verbal communication, exploration of feelings, and using and interpreting body language were designed with older children in mind.

Usually gross language problems that might have originally caused the child to be isolated from his peer group are no longer evident in intermediate grades. But the language requirements for older children are infinitely more complex and become an intrinsic part of their personality. It is essential then that subtle deficits not be overlooked and that remediation programs (which can serve as enrichment for the abler students) be initiated.

Further Considerations

The older child is not so quick to reflect the teacher's attitudes toward his classmates. In fact, if a teacher is very negative toward a child whom the group likes, they may show anger toward the teacher. Peer approval becomes more and more important and authority approval less so as the child matures. Nevertheless, it is still necessary that the teacher serve as a model of fairness and, particularly important, as a reflector of self-worth for the children. If she shows respect and attention to their thoughts and ideas, even the loneliest children will begin to feel that what they have to offer is important and worthwhile. As the teacher demonstrates concern and listens to the children, so then will they begin to listen more respectfully to one another. Hopefully, she will also be using the teaching materials that have been designed to foster thoughtful and considered discussions and interactions, and to enhance the substance and interest value of the group's communications. As these children learn to express deeper, more meaningful feelings, develop an enlarged repertoire of ideas to share, and learn that being a good listener is a valued asset in the total process of social interaction, their peers will more readily join them in the mature, sociocentric, *collaborative* aspects of communication.

THE ROLE OF JUNIOR- AND SENIOR-HIGH SCHOOL TEACHERS

By the time a student reaches high school age, he is expected to have mastered reasonably well the social skills required of his age group. Teachers on this level are relatively subject oriented—their college training has generally emphasized academics rather than child development—'and they do not expect to be concerned with problems of loneliness in their students. They may go so far as to refer "problem" children to guidance counselors, but their real job, as they see it, is to make certain that their pupils learn the English, math, foreign language, or history in which they have been so arduously trained. This section is being written with the hope that some of these teachers,* recognizing the acute pain felt by the "outsiders" in their classes, will look for some way to salve these hurts.

Making Referrals and Recommendations

In the higher grades, it cannot be expected that math (or science or English) teachers take time out to begin a program in communications and social skills. We *can* expect that they will at least recognize the child who is lonely, or worse, ostracized, and try to traffic this young person toward sources of help. At the least, they can take a few minutes to describe the problem to a guidance person in the school. If such ancillary services are not available, then an appointment with the child's parents to tell them of one's concern is an appropriate step.

It would be especially helpful to the young person and his parents if the teacher makes an effort to find available sources of help and information. He might recommend appropriate books or, through contact with a local university's psychology or special education department, learn of agencies and parent groups that can serve the lonely youngster. If he takes the time to become more knowledgeable in the field, he can counsel the parents with some of the ideas mentioned in chapter seven of this book.

Effecting Positive Attitudes

Although the classroom cannot be the place for remedial training, it can be a place where the youngster finds an accepting group

---

* Those who teach special classes on this level generally are dealing with young people functioning well below average expectancy levels in subject areas and, therefore, are not absolutely bound to the normal track curriculum. They should be able to make good use of the many suggested instructional activities described in this chapter and in Part 4, which, although geared to the intermediate level, are equally applicable to lower functioning older students.

of people. The teacher is in a position to talk to the class (when the lonely child is not present) and hopefully turn cruel gibes to kinder words and feelings.

When he recognizes a lonely child, the teacher can of course (no matter what subject area he teaches) utilize some of the previously mentioned methods for pairing this youngster with a warm and friendly peer (see earlier portions of this chapter). Any positive experiences a lonely young person enjoys can help to counteract at least some of the unhappy negative ones he has already lived through. A concerned teacher can even try to pave the way toward more acceptance in other classes by sharing some of his interest and feelings with the youngster's other instructors.

Expanding the Curriculum

Perhaps, as more attention and interest is engendered by specialists in education and psychology toward the plight of lonely young people, a course of study in communications can be instituted. Probably teachers of English are best prepared to undertake such a venture. In teaching their students understanding of the characterizations in short stories, novels, and plays, they are, in effect, dealing with human psychology. They already teach speech courses; it is not too farfetched, then, to envision a course that can help the socially inept to communicate more effectively. The secondary school's syllabus can also be expanded to include such subjects as philosophy (ethical considerations, empathy) and psychology (self-awareness, problems of adolescence) in hopes that the unhappy and lonely adolescent will be better understood and will function in a more relaxed, confident, and productive fashion.

REFERENCES

Cedoline, Anthony J. *The Effect of Affect*. San Rafael, Calif.: Academic Therapy Publications, 1977.

Flaste, Richard. "Life on the Sidelines: The Lonely Children." *The New York Times* (*Parents/Children syndicated column*), January 14, 1977.

New York City Board of Education, Division of Educational Planning and Support, *Oral Communication: Grades K-6*, Curriculum Bulletin, 1976–1977 Series, No. 2.

PART 4

Strengthening Social Perceptions

In the organization of remedial activities, we have chosen to proceed along the lines of task orientation *rather than* process orientation. *In other words, we do not attempt to zero in on corrective methodologies for central processes such as visual perception, body image, and spatial orientation, nor do we meet head on such traits as egocentricity, concretism, and perseveration. Our strategy, instead,* is *to regard* observable behavior, *that is, the actual deficits in receiving and expressing nonverbal communication signals (and attendant deficits in conversational skills), and set forth a task-related program for improvement.*

We believe that many of the theorized causes of poor social perception can be reached more readily indirectly via correcting some particular aspect of body language or conversational skill. For example, it is easier to learn to pantomime such messages as "I can't hear you," "Go away," "You better be careful," or "I'm overjoyed" than it is to acquire reliable body image. Similarly, correcting a child's tendency to ignore a third party can be addressed directly without aiming to correct incidental learning deficiencies or perceptual problems in general.

Moreover, in the very act of practicing some specific nonverbal communication skill, the possible underlying causes are also being tapped. The student who is learning how to play charades is, since he is participating with others, also learning to be less egocentric. Practice in detecting the vocal tones denoting sarcasm is, in effect, an example of auditory perceptual training. The game of "Twenty Questions" nurtures logical thought processes.

In this part, no attempt is made to categorize remedial activities dealing with expression as distinct from those entailing reception. The same activity is often applicable to both—for instance, the game "The Manner of the Adverb" involves both acting (expressing) *and guessing* (receiving) *nonverbal messages.*

CHAPTER 9

Improving Body Language

Pantomiming entails the conveying of messages via actions instead of words. These actions may involve body movement and posture, gesture, and/or facial expression (including eye movement). For a message in pantomime to be successfully negotiated, the *sender* must possess skill in using body language effectively. He must be able to demonstrate surprise by opening his mouth; suspicion by looking over his shoulder; nervousness by drumming his fingers on the table; disagreement by shaking his head; puzzlement by arching his eyebrows; boredom by drooping of eyelids, frequent shifting of body position, and glancing at his wristwatch; depression by slumping and drooping the muscles around the mouth. He must be able to show the appropriate gesture for such thoughts as "Come with me," "Later," "Right here," "I don't know," "I disapprove," "You smell bad," "Hold everything!" and "Please continue." Beyond this, he must wait for the "audience" to watch, he must plan his actions rather than plunge into them impulsively, and must apply some degree of logic in deciding which set of gestures to use.

Reciprocally, the *receiver* must be able to interpret the various units of pantomime. In addition, he, too, must attend, organize, avoid being overly concrete (after all, a frown—especially a feigned one—is only a *symbol* for anger, it is not *actual* anger), must wait for enough cues rather than blurt out wild guesses, and—like the sender—must think in an organized, logical fashion. The activities that follow are worthwhile educationally, in themselves, in that, by participating in them, the individual receives the guided experience he needs to develop nonverbal communication skills. Moreover, they can serve as a springboard into other facets of training involving *corrective* nonverbal communication designed to render one more adept in expressing and/or receiving designated messages—especially messages of *feeling* such as hostility, disgust, disinterest, despair, and enthusiasm. Some of these aspects of training are: evaluation, analysis, and labeling of movements; isolating a particular gesture or movement for more extensive drill; demonstration (by the teacher, parent, or a classmate adept in body language) of an acceptable pantomime model; choosing the appropriate gesture and movements from a set of related ones; and selective practice.

CHARADES. One person (or team) decides upon a slogan, proverb, or title of a book, poem, song, TV show, or movie. He then acts it out and the other person (or team) must guess the answer. There are a variety of acceptable methods for conveying the selected message:

1. *Act out every word.* In "Ol' Man River," *old* can be pantomimed by walking in a stooped position using an imaginary walking cane. *Man* can be expressed by simply pointing to a man (or, if none is present, to a boy, and then gesturing "later" or "bigger"). *River* can be denoted by pretending to swim, to row a boat, or by rolling up one's trousers and simulating wading.

2. *Act out the important words only.* In "Call of the Wild," it may only be necessary to act out *call* and *wild*.

3. *Break the words into syllables.* "Robinson Crusoe" can be approached by *rob, in, sun, crew,* and *sew*.

4. *Act out the entire message.* "Oh, What a Beautiful Morning" may be depicted by pantomiming arising from sleep, rubbing one's eyes, pulling up a window shade, looking at the view, and wearing a rapturous expression.

110

The commercial version of Charades introduces additional signals: Touching one's nose means "on the nose," that is, the receiver guessed the right word. Tugging at one's ear signifies "sounds like," that is, the sender may wish to pantomime a rhyming word—for example, *money* instead of *funny* in "Funny Girl." There is a preconveyed signal for *book* (pretending to read), *movie* (turning one's hand in a cranking motion pretending to be taking a motion picture), *song* (pretending to sing), and so on. The number of words, the number of syllables, the specific word or syllable (first, second, third) to be acted out can all be shown by holding up the appropriate number of fingers.

A helpful modification might be to have a list of some of the common words that are difficult to act out (for example, *the, a, an, with, than, it*) printed on a chart and simply point to them when needed.

Charades need not be confined to the above. Hennings (1974, Chapter II) suggests activities that include the pantomiming of individual words—*crept, sneaked, hobbled, swaggered, confused, bored, unhappy;* shapes—the shapes of some of the alphabet letters, the shapes of animals such as an elephant or giraffe; motion—of animals such as a snake crawling or a horse galloping, of objects such as an eggbeater, of playing musical instruments; and situations—brushing one's teeth, playing Ping-Pong, threading a needle, suffering from a toothache, trying to drive off a bothersome fly, trying not to sneeze. Some of these, like the letter *F,* can be formed by an individual, whereas more complicated forms may require several people.

In addition to these, there are the theatrical kinds of situations, which almost anyone can do with a little practice. These include: pulling an imaginary big, frisky, and at times uncooperative dog on a leash; simulating carrying a heavy package; several individuals pushing a stalled car; playing a tug-of-war game (without the rope, of course). All of these situations are broad rather than subtle, slapstick, in essence, and go for the big guffaw. Their high "fun index" suggests that they might well be introductory to an overall program for pantomiming, particularly for younger, inexperienced pupils.

In Charades, as in any other pantomiming activity, it is possible to select messages that convey feelings as well as those that merely convey thoughts, ideas, memories, images of *neutral* objects or occurrences. (There is not much emotion in pretending that you are the letter *T* or that you are sharpening a pencil or taking off your shoe.) Nevertheless, the neutral theme has value in that its messages are usually easier to perform. This is true from two standpoints: (1) physically (it's easier to pretend to be swinging a baseball bat than to feign being in love) and (2) psychologically (a child is less likely to be self-conscious about simulating an elephant walking than when pantomiming anger). These nonemotional items may well serve to "loosen up" players who are somewhat anxious and reticent.

However, since our total thrust is toward helping those who are unable readily to perceive (and to express) nonverbal cues of attitudes, intentions, and moods, teachers—or parents—should have a pool of feeling-conveying messages from which to draw. Hopefully, they will be familiar with such titles as "Twelve *Angry* Men," "*Happy* Days Are Here Again," "*Pride* and Prejudice," "Who's *Sorry* Now?" "Who's *Afraid* of Virginia Woolf?" "I'll Never *Smile* Again," and "Do You *Love* Me?"

In addition to titles that depict feeling, the teacher should have in mind a number of emotion-packed situations such as being stuck in traffic and growing more impatient, walking through a dark, deserted alley, expecting F's but receiving all A's on your report card, finding (or losing) a lot of money, finding an oasis on a desert, not knowing any of the answers on a test, sneaking home late at night, forgetting your lines in a school play, being lost in a foreign country, getting a haircut from a barber whose hands are noticeably shaking. Individual feeling-laden words for pantomiming include: *disappointed, frightened, glad, disgusted, bored, shy, stare, strut, wince,* and of course such expletives as *Wow! Oh! ouch!* and *ahh!*

An excellent introduction to Charades is to set aside a block of time, usually from five to ten minutes, wherein communication is permissible and, in fact, encouraged *but absolutely no talking is allowed.* For example, the teacher can knock on her desk to get the class's attention, hold up the arithmetic book, then, by holding up the correct number of fingers (say, three "tens" and a "four") signify page thirty-four. Next, she holds up three fingers and immediately afterward points to example three on that page. The children now know that they must do that example. The teacher can tap one student, give him a stack of paper and pantomime that he is to distribute them. One student may raise his hand, point to the door, then simulate drinking. The teacher shakes her head no and holds up two fingers ("You can't get a drink now, but I'll let you go in two minutes"). The student may protest by panting ("I'm very thirsty") and frowning ("I'm very uncomfortable"), whereupon the teacher may relent and signal him to get his drink of water now.

This particular game is unusual in that normal classroom procedures continue throughout—except that *no one, not even the teacher, is allowed to talk.* It gets the students used to the notion of pantomiming. It is absolutely nonthreatening, since no one pupil is compelled to send messages; if a child chooses, he can simply observe (and enjoy) the various pantomime messages that are going on around him. Finally, the messages themselves are all nonemotional in nature and hence can be seen as preparatory for some of the more "feeling" messages of Charades.

THE MANNER OF THE ADVERB. One child leaves the room. The others decide upon some adverb, for example, *nervously.* He is then called back and begins picking individuals—one at a time— to perform specific actions in the manner of the selected adverb: for example, "John, dance in the manner of the adverb," "Helen, sew in the manner of the adverb," "Fred, eat in the manner of the adverb," "Irene, walk in the manner of the adverb." (For less advanced pupils, the word *adverb* may be omitted entirely. Simply select a word that tells *"how* a person can do something." The guesser then says, "John, dance that way.") He continues to call for a new action—or another person to perform some prior one— until he guesses the adverb. It is a good idea to allow synonyms to count as a correct answer. In the illustrated case, *anxiously, tensely,* and *up-tight* would all be scored correct.

For variation, several children—instead of one—can be the guessers. This has the advantage of reducing embarrassment; that is, the lengthy interlude in which no answer—or only incorrect ones—come forth is shared and no one child is placed under the spotlight. Moreover, it encourages social intercourse—listening, considering other's views, explaining, persuading—inasmuch as a joint decision must be reached.

Some adverbs can best be acted out when applied to a particular action. In such cases, an effective variation of the game would be to provide a hint to the guesser. Suppose the adverb is *sloppily*. If the guesser orders a player to "sing in the manner of the adverb" or to "sleep in the manner of the adverb," it will be difficult to convey *sloppily*. It is appropriate at that point to suggest that the guesser ask someone to "eat in the manner of the adverb," thus facilitating the communication of that particular adverb. Similarly, it is easier to *write* suspiciously than to *breathe* suspiciously; to *walk* stealthily than to *sing* stealthily; to *sleep* peacefully, than to *clap hands* peacefully.

The astute teacher will realize that in this game, as in Charades, there are emotional messages (angrily, fearfully, romantically, calmly, nervously, disgustedly, longingly, disdainfully, proudly, excitedly, sadly, etc.) and neutral ones (quickly, slowly, suddenly, noisily, carefully, drunkenly, etc.) to be communicated. In many instances it will be sound pedagogy to structure this activity by providing initial experiences in nonfeeling adverbs. Later, as the players become less self-conscious, the more emotional words can be introduced.

WHAT AM I SAYING? In this game, described by Hennings (1974, 59–60), three sets of related sentences are written on the board (or a chart). A player chooses one from a given set to act out. The others must watch him and try to guess the message. The illustrative examples suggested are:

> He was very attentive.
> He paid no attention.
> He paid only a little attention.
>
> He enjoyed what was going on.
> He hated every moment of it.
> He was only half-hearted about what was going on.

114

The little girl was afraid of the dog.
The little girl loved the dog.
The little girl ignored the dog.

I am disgusted.
I am proud.
I am angry.

Less advanced pupils (that is, those who are relatively socially imperceptive, more concrete, less imaginative) should be given the background and/or setting along with the triad of choices. For example, the one dealing with attention could begin with "Helen is your neighbor and friend of the family. She approaches you and begins telling you about her recent trip to Canada. How would you act?" Then give these three choices: (1) I am extremely interested in what you are saying, (2) I'm not really interested but I'll try to look polite, (3) I'm bored with you and I don't care who knows it. For these children, it is well-advised, initially at least, to have them portray the different actions *while maintaining their own identity,* hence the use of the first person *I.* Still another supportive modification is, in the beginning, to make the language more dramatic, more directive, and therefore more suggestive of specific actions.

The one concerning enjoyment could read:

"You're watching a school play."
a. I'm really enjoying it very much.
b. I hate every minute of this.
c. I can take this or leave it—it's just OK.

The situation about the dog could read:

"You are visiting a house that has a very large dog you have never seen before."
a. I am afraid of this dog.
b. I like this dog very much.
c. I'm not interested in dogs.

The last example might be modified by:

"You are a parent who is seeing your child's first report card of the year."

115

a. I am disgusted with your terrible marks.
b. I am very proud of you because you got all A's.
c. I am very angry with you because you got such bad marks in conduct.

Hennings (1974, 60–61) has similar activities listed under the heading "Body Talk." In all of these illustrations, the author provides the setting:

- Believe you are washing windows.
  Let your body say you are really trying to do a good job.
  Let your body say you hate the job.
  Let your body say that you are rushing the job to get to something else.

- Believe you are standing in line.
  Let your body say you are waiting to have a flu shot.
  Let your body say you are waiting to go to an exciting movie and you can hardly wait.
  Let your body say you are tired of waiting.

- Believe you are chopping wood.
  Let your body say that you are very tired, but you are determined to get the job done anyway.
  Let your body say that you have lots of energy and are eager to do the job. You enjoy it.
  Let your body say that you are being required to do the task and you don't like it.

- Believe you are listening to a person speak to you.
  Let your body say that you disagree violently with the speaker.
  Let your body say you are really in agreement with the speaker.
  Let your body say you are having trouble staying awake.

The "choice" aspect of this activity adds to its novelty, thereby fostering interest and motivation. In addition, it parallels real life situations, since, in experiences involving social negotiations of any kind, there is a given theme (the overall, *apparent* transaction, that is, the words themselves) against which any of a number of variations (one's true feelings about it) may be played. Reciprocally, the socially imperceptive observer in a real life situation usually has relatively little difficulty in understanding the gross,

116

surface transaction; rather, he falls down in interpreting the subtle variations—the underlying, real message of intent and mood.

SKITS IN PANTOMIME. Two or more pupils are selected and must, without speaking any words, act out a given skit while the rest of the class observe and try to guess what is happening. The skits can involve such situations as buying a pair of shoes, taking a very difficult spelling test, getting stuck in a crowded elevator, being examined by a doctor, borrowing something from a neighbor, conducting a job interview. The entire drama can be planned prior to the performance or it may be improvised.

"One-man shows" may also be used effectively. Situations can be created that call for portrayal by a single individual. A game format can be utilized in which the teacher or parent provides various "scripts," each one on a separate index card. One player selects one of the cards, reads it, and pantomimes it while the others watch and try to interpret his actions. The successful guesser becomes the next actor.

Some suggested situations are:

1. Pour a glass of milk (juice, etc.) and drink it.
2. Walk into a room. See a robber. Then put up your hands. (Be sure to look scared.)
3. Cut up your steak. Keep cutting, then put some into your mouth. Chew and swallow.
4. Read a book.
5. Turn on the TV set. Tune to a channel. Then watch it.
6. Shine an apple. Then begin eating it. Chew and swallow.
7. Peel a banana and eat it.
8. Be up at bat and then hit a home run.
9. Mount and ride a two-wheeled bicycle.
10. Make a phone call in a pay phone.
11. Wash your hair in the sink and then dry it.
12. Watch a movie (stare) while you eat popcorn.
13. Break a dish. Sweep up the mess and put it into the garbage pail.
14. Jump rope.

15. Be a big, fat bear. Find some honey and begin eating. Then bees sting you.
16. Put on your socks and shoes. Tie the laces.
17. Put a record on. Then listen and sway (or dance) to the music.
18. Be a prizefighter.
19. Lean a tall ladder against the wall. Begin climbing up. As you climb higher and higher, you get scared.
20. Call a cat to you. Begin petting it. Then it scratches you.

Carol Even in Furth and Wachs (1975, 247–248) suggests several extensions of the one-man skit:

What Am I Doing?
One player pantomimes a simple activity—frying an egg, hitting a baseball, going down a slide. The teacher asks volunteers to join the first player one at a time and do the same activity. When five to ten players are doing the pantomime the players "freeze." Starting with the most recent joiners to the game and working his way to the first player last, the teacher asks each child what he is doing (some may not be doing the original activity but one that uses a similar motion). Finally the first player is asked what he was doing. Usually no discussion is needed after the game.

What Are We Doing?
One player pantomimes a simple activity, as above (making toast, catching the ball). The teacher asks volunteers to join the first player one at a time and do a related activity. (For example: Player A is talking on the telephone. B pantomimes talking to A with another telephone. C sits between as the telephone operator. D and E also become operators. The teacher then says, "Let's have someone else now. Someone doing something new in the scene.")
Discussion: Do you do that the same way he did? How else could it be done? Could all of those people have been there in real life? Who else might have been in that scene and what would he have been doing?

Another way of creating pantomime roles is to stipulate a given setting, for example, a playground (New York City Board of Education, 1976–1977, 65). One child begins to pantomime some action appropriate to that environment. If, upon viewing the performance, a pupil recognizes that the action is supposed to be taking place in a playground, he "enters" and begins doing something else that can also portray playground behavior. Other children join accordingly. Additional examples of specific settings are a ballpark, a library, a cafeteria, an office.

From the standpoint of structure, the number of actors should be limited initially. Gradually, as the pupils become accustomed to playing this game, more can be added. In some instances, when it is not too unwieldy, the entire class can become active participants.

Another format that involves the active participation of the entire class in pantomiming is suggested by Furth and Wachs (1975, 248):

Mates
The class is divided in half. A different simple activity is given to each child in team A: bouncing a ball, rolling out pie dough, putting on makeup, breaking eggs, painting a fence, setting a table, painting a scene on an easel, sewing, chopping wood. The same list of simple activities is given out to the members of team B. No one knows what anyone else's activity is. Team A spreads out in a line or a circle and begins to pantomime their activities. Team B observes. As a member of team B recognizes his assigned activity, he joins his mate from team A and they do their activity standing together.

Discussion: Did your mate do your activity the same way you did? What did he do that made you recognize that he was your mate? Is there another way to do that activity? How? Show us.

This activity entails pupil-pupil interaction, an essential ingredient in extending sociocentric thinking and concomitant socialization skills. Moreover, it can serve to nourish a more positive self-concept: Within each given team, the role of any pupil is unique and, even more importantly, he is actually being sought and singled out.

FILMSTRIPS AND SILENT MOVIES. Wiig and Semel (1976, 312–313) believe that filmstrips and silent movies (dubbing out all written words) are excellent sources for training in social perception since they present dynamic, sequential visual stimuli. The authors advise that initially the films selected should consist of body language that is overstated and unambiguous. Later ones should portray less exaggerated actions. Finally, those containing ambiguities may be introduced. Wiig and Semel (313) describe one such film—originally developed for therapy with adult aphasics—in which two adolescents "square off," apparently ready to fight. They face each other with clenched fists—but they are smiling. Immediately after, they are seen walking away with their arms around each other's shoulders. Hence, it is finally apparent that they were only fooling. The authors point out that learning disabled youngsters frequently focus on a single aspect of the total set of body language cues (in this case, the face *or* the fists), thus missing the ambiguity. Hence they misinterpret the true intention of the actors and will be unable to anticipate the actual outcome. Verbal labeling of the cues (for example, calling attention to—and naming—the smile) and allowing the ambiguity to resolve (rather than leave it hanging) are means by which the ability to perceive and interpret nonverbal communication messages may improve.

Alternatives to silent movies, if they are not readily available, would be a sound movie, a TV play, or a videotape, all with the sound turned down. Drama majors from local colleges may wish to volunteer their talents—perhaps in conjunction with a course they are taking. They could visit a class periodically, say, once weekly, creating and performing wordless plays, discussing their body language, and coaching the pupils in receiving and expressing nonverbal communication signals. An extension of watching wordless movies (or plays) would be for the class actually to produce its own.

FACIAL EXPRESSION ACTIVITIES. Facial expression may very well be the "bottom line" of body language. When we surmise someone's emotional state by his appearance, isn't it usually the facial expression that is of prime importance? This is not to downgrade the other elements of body language such as posture and gesture, and, in fact, the message is strengthened when all these signals are congruent. Nevertheless, if we have to narrow it down to *one* source, the nonverbal cue that suggests to us that an individual is either happy or despondent, fearful or calm, excited or nonchalant, accepting or rejecting of us, interested or bored, it would most likely be the facial expression. It is no coincidence that we generally look at the face of the one with whom we are speaking. True, the feedback derived from lipreading and from facing the direct source of sound helps, but probably more important is eye contact (eye movements are a vital part of facial expression) and overall facial scanning.

In all instruction—especially in the case of handicapped learners—the structure offered by a sequential approach is most important. Just as practice in observing and understanding the nonverbal communication of a single person should precede an attempt to derive meaning from social situations that are more complex (Johnson and Myklebust, 1967, 297), acquiring proficiency in sending and receiving signals via facial expression should come before other elements of nonverbal communication. Training would include:

Practicing making appropriate facial expression in a mirror.

Matching the expression you make in a mirror with a model (a picture or drawing, the teacher's or another pupil's expression).

Deciding whether two expressions (actual or of pictures) are the same or different.

Analyzing and labeling of the various facial expressions (frown, smirk, puzzlement, determination).

Catching the pupil in a particular frame of mind and calling his attention to his facial expression at that time, perhaps with the aid of a Polaroid camera (Johnson and Myklebust, 1967, 297).

Matching facial expressions (select the correct photograph and/or assume the correct facial expression) with given settings (for example, "You're getting a tooth pulled," "You just received a new toy," "You just found out that your best friend is coming to see you," "You're talking to someone who has bad breath").

121

Making up stories to go with a given facial expression (a draw-ing, photograph, or an actual facial expression).

Recognizing incongruities between what one is saying and his facial expression.

Looking at eye expression only and guessing the entire facial expression. (Cover the rest of the face, but expose only the rectangular patch—about one third of the entire facial area —that includes the eyes. Photographs and/or the face of an actual person may be used. When working with live models, the teacher is preferable to a young pupil—since a child may have difficulty maintaining a given facial ex-pression.)

Matching facial expressions with captions. (Arrange a series of portraits, each depicting a different facial expression, and each captioned with a brief quotation. Some will not fit— for example, a smiling face may be captioned with "Ouch! that hurts!" whereas others will be correctly matched. The task is to decide whether or not each caption fits its portrait and to correct those that do not. The corrections can at first be made by simply switching some of the captions. Later, the child can be required to compose original ones.)

Drawing facial expressions.* Children need not be particularly talented in art in order to learn how to make very simplified drawings of facial expressions. The teacher will achieve best results here by proceeding sequentially: (1) draw a circle, (2) fill in eyes as dots, and the mouth and eyebrows as slightly curved lines, (3) proceed to happy faces (upturned mouths) and sad faces (downturned mouths), (4) grad-ually introduce additional emotions and add several fea-tures: tears, anger lines, wide-open or half-closed eyes, and so on.

In learning to draw facial expressions, the class gets a better handle on nonverbal communication—receptively as well as ex-pressively. Moreover, it is a form of creativity and self-expression, especially if they are encouraged to write original captions to go

* We are indebted to Sandra Gart for suggesting this activity and for supplying the artwork.

Pleasure　　　　　　　　　　　　　　　　　　*Anger*

Surprise

Sadness　　　　　　　　　　　　　　　　　　*Boredom*

with their drawings. The senior author visited a regular fourth-grade class that was engaged in this activity. One pupil drew a bored face and wrote, as caption, "I'm good in math and my teacher keeps teaching zero take away zero!"

Frequently, individuals who are poor in nonverbal communication have adequate verbal abilities. This may well be the key to training. Johnson and Myklebust (1967, 296–297) believe that

> training in social perception requires verbalization and interpretation of the nonverbal world. It seems that children with impaired social perception cannot understand visual nonverbal experiences until they are translated into verbal symbols. . . . they cannot look and comprehend, but through verbalization they learn to understand. Therefore, we capitalize on their verbal facility and arrange

123

meaningful experiences. It is impossible to anticipate all of the events in the child's world, but the training is geared toward helping him establish a frame of reference; its purpose is to give him a means of scanning the environment systematically, while noting relationships and internally verbalizing what he observes.

Hence, central to any training program designed to strengthen social perception—and expression—would be activities involving analyzing and evaluating verbally, describing, defining, and labeling of the various nonverbal communication cues.

REFERENCES

Furth, Hans G., and Wachs, Harry. *Thinking Goes to School: Piaget's Theory in Practice.* New York: Oxford University Press, 1975.

Hennings, Dorothy Grant. *Smiles, Nods, and Pauses.* New York: Citation Press, 1974.

Johnson, Doris, and Myklebust, Helmer. *Learning Disabilities: Educational Principles and Practices.* New York: Grune and Stratton, 1967.

New York City Board of Education, Division of Educational Planning and Support, *Oral Communication, Grades K–6,* Curriculum Bulletin, 1976–1977 Series, No. 2.

Wiig, Elisabeth H., and Semel, Eleanor Messing. *Language Disabilities in Children and Adolescents.* Columbus, Ohio: Charles E. Merrill Co., 1976.

CHAPTER 10

Improving Conversational Skills

COMMUNICATING WITH INTEREST

The lonely child is often rejected because he is not interested—or, at least, does not show interest—in others. The reasons for this are manifold and have already been discussed (for instance, distractibility, egocentricity, anxiety, perceptual impairment). Training activities can be designed that provide children with specific instruction (cues, strategies, etc.) for attending to others and for showing greater interest in what others are saying. Granted, the very idea of making the classroom lesson the format for mastering that which comes "naturally" to most children seems somewhat artificial. Nevertheless, there are distinct advantages to this approach: The practice can be graded in complexity and meted out in appropriate time dosages. The teacher is in position to supervise, correct, and structure. She can advise the parents on how to provide further social perception experiences outside of school. Finally, she is there to support—and shelter—the lonely child through this initial stage, which is a crucial one since his rejection is at its height; as conversational skills increase, so will his acceptability. The activities that follow are designed to help such children learn to show greater interest in—and indeed, to become interested in—others.

What Did He (She) Say?

Let two children converse informally. In the beginning, you may have to give them a specific topic (a recent assembly play, a popular TV show, vacation plans, "the teacher I had last year," "my favorite school subject") in order to help them get started. After a designated time, say, two minutes, ring a bell. This signals them to stop immediately. The one who is listening must be able to tell you what the other child just said (that is, his last statement). Do not tell them the purpose of this game in advance, only that at some point after they commence talking, you will ring a bell, they are to stop, and you will have a question to ask. After the first trial(s), they may surmise—or you may explicitly tell them—that in order to "win," they must really listen to the speaker even though they will, at the same time, be thinking about what they are going to say. By not informing the participants of the game's purpose initially, the "pretest"-"posttest" format is maintained, the difference in performances will likely be greater, hence any improvement can more readily be noted by the teacher and, even more importantly, by the children themselves.

In a classroom, a single pair of pupils may participate while the rest of the class serves as audience; the entire class can be divided into pairs and play the game simultaneously; still another format is to arrange the class into groups of three, the third individual acting as monitor. A tape recorder can help since it can verify the pupil's answer.

Getting to Know You

Give a pair of children a very specific topic of conversation. Choose one in which they both are interested (for example, softball vs. punchball as a school sport, why younger siblings are a pain, is the TV character "Fonz" more interesting than "Kotter"?). The purpose of this activity—which should last from three to five minutes (timed)—is that each child learns something about the person with whom he is conversing.

126

Initially, the points of information to be discovered are assigned by the teacher (in secret) to each child and should be directly related to the conversational topic: For example, if they are talking about sports, the questions might include: "Have you ever seen a live game?" "Do you belong to Little League?" When the children become more familiar and more comfortable with the game, the assigned topics need not be of the simple, factual type, but can become more attitudinal, personal, and more emotionally laden ("When was the last time you cried?" "How do you feel about your last year's teacher?" "What things make you angry?")

The teacher should instruct the pupils that not only must they garner some information about one another, but that each must remain unaware of what *specific* information the other has been seeking. Therefore, they must gradually learn how to work the question into the conversation unobtrusively and they must continue to converse even after the goal has been reached. The latter is facilitated by allotting a prearranged time span. (A kitchen timer helps.)

For some children, it might be useful for a teacher aide and the teacher, or for two team-teachers to illustrate this activity. In this beginning stage, the children can be involved in choosing the conversational topic and in proposing the information to be learned. The general format is for the two children to converse in front of the class. However, some may be too shy for this, and so, initially, they can talk with only the teacher as audience, into a tape recorder, or even privately, later reporting the results to the teacher.

The long-range goal is for the child to learn to express interest in the person with whom he is talking. An egocentric individual talks *at* his audience; effective communication demands a "talking *with*" style.

Who Is Listening?

Instruct one pupil to relate something to two classmates. The topic should be such that it lends itself to a discourse of about two to three minutes. The topics can be of a personal nature: my most embarrassing moment, my family, things that frighten me, my best friend, what I like most and least about school. They can also reflect the individual's beliefs: the greatest president, marijuana should be legalized, how to stop violence in professional hockey games. In advance of the conversation, the two listeners are instructed (and coached) in how to act. One is to pretend that he is extremely interested, while the other simulates abject boredom. At some prearranged signal, the conversation is ended and the speaker is asked to identify the interested listener and the bored one, and to tell how he made his decision.

This activity should be preceded by—and followed up with—identifying facial expressions of photographs and/or pictures, assuming bored and interested expressions with and without the use of a mirror, describing how a bored person looks and acts as contrasted with one who is interested, acting either bored or interested wearing a mask (thus calling attention to the body language aspects of communicating these two emotions), making simplified drawings of bored and interested faces, and so on.

Later, the teacher can increase the number of listeners. The speaker must now make many observations and judgments. Which two people were most interested? Which one person was bored through and through? Who started out interested and then became bored? Another supportive method is to start by having the listeners communicate their emotions without speaking; later, they are allowed to join the conversation but only perfunctorily (for example, the bored pupil may wish simply to grunt "hmm" occasionally, whereas the interested party urges the speaker to continue with an eager "yeah, yeah").

The purpose of this activity is to help the speaker learn to differentiate the two reactions: interest and boredom. This will serve as a springboard into how to take the listener's attitude into consideration and how to modify his own communication behavior when needed. He needs to find the answers to such questions as, "How can I continue to hold his interest?" "How can I change what I'm saying and/or the manner in which I am saying it to make him less bored?" "Should I stop talking?" "Should I ask him how he feels about what I'm saying?" and most importantly, "How can I encourage him to take part in the conversation?" Clearly, the teacher's knowledge of the subject matter (that is, the overall area of nonverbal communication), her expertise as a teacher, her own enthusiasm and creativity, the degree to which she accepts, can empathize with, and show sensitivity toward those who are socially imperceptive and lonely are essential factors that can contribute toward significant growth in this area. Such teaching activities as questions and answers, discussions, enumerating those features that enable us to recognize whether an individual is bored or interested, setting up (and listing on a chart) guidelines for communicating in an interesting and interested manner, analyzing brief scripts or portions of scripts to determine their interest index are all appropriate. Additional activities could include listening to tape recordings of brief conversations in order to determine (from the context as well as from the manner of speech) whether or not one character showed interest in another; watching portions of TV "soap operas" and talk shows and identifying portrayals of boredom and of interest; or stopping a class skit at some random point and instructing one of the players to change his style (that is, if he was interested up to this point, he must now simulate boredom, and vice versa).

What Do They Think of Me?

This activity is essentially like the previous one—*Who Is Listening?* The chief difference is that, instead of staying with the interest-boredom duo only, other emotions are introduced. Some of these will be paired opposites: nervous-relaxed, anger-acceptance. Single ones may also be used: disgust, surprise, shock, pride. It is extremely important to proceed sequentially starting with prepared scripts that lend themselves handily to some of the suggested emotional expressions. (One example would be for the speaker to discuss his recent report card grades. Obviously this could elicit disgust, surprise, pride, and the like. Another would be for him to describe all the foods he ate at a recent wedding.) Later, only the topic need be suggested. Finally the pupils may create their own scripts as they go along.

Again, the purposes of this activity are (1) to teach children to recognize a particular emotion and to adjust their conversation accordingly, and (2) to become more effective in conveying their emotions nonverbally.

Say It Differently

Select a pupil. Tell him to present his point of view concerning a controversial topic to a classmate. Some suggested topics are: schools should be open all year round, no homework should be given, corporal punishment should be allowed, we should not have to raise our hand when we want to speak, tests should not be given, no one should be on welfare if he refuses to work, and capital punishment should be outlawed. The classmate should be instructed to take the opposite point of view. An informal debate ensues. The purpose of this activity is to encourage the pupil to state his position, *listen to the opposing view, then restate his position, but taking into account the other person's view.* In short, it gets to the heart of the *collaborative* quality of communication.

An unacceptable dialogue follows:

JOHN: I don't think we should have any homework. We spend a lot of time in school. When we get home, it's much better for our health to rest and to play outdoors than to have to do a lot of homework.

HENRY: You can rest and play outdoors a lot on weekends, vacations, and holidays. Homework is very important so you can learn a lot and go to college and get a good job when you grow up.

JOHN: Yes, but I'm saying that it's much better for our health to rest and play outdoors instead of doing a lot of homework.

Here's an acceptable dialogue:

JOHN: (the same)
HENRY: (the same)
JOHN: Yes, but I'm saying that I don't think weekends and vacations are enough. We need rest and fresh air and exercise every day. Besides, if the school didn't waste so much time on things like assembly programs and trips, we could learn more during the day.

Clearly, in the first version, John did not respond to Henry's ideas at all. He said, "Yes, but I'm saying . . . ," and then proceeded to repeat the very words that, only a moment ago, failed to convince Henry! In the second round, he addressed himself to Henry's argument, countering with ". . . weekends and vacations aren't enough." He then went on to bolster his own view by pointing out that more teaching *could* go on during the school day if frills were eliminated.

It is highly likely that Henry enjoyed the latter conversation more than the unacceptable sample: Even though it is an argument, his statements are not being ignored.

Much practice should be devoted to this activity. At first, pairs of pupils can talk, later the group can be enlarged. Initially, the teacher will have to suggest a topic, but afterward, the pupils could select their own. It might even help to allow the pupils to outline their points of view prior to the discussion and to talk from notes. As they become more adept at this, the notes need not be used, and finally, the dialogue can be performed extemporaneously.

Another variation is for the entire conversation to unfold as a written exercise. That is, Jane writes her opening statement, Henry reads it and writes his response, then Jane writes *her* reaction to Henry's point, and so forth. Some dialogues can be prepared on cassettes, or totally in written form for a more mature class. The object there would be to analyze, evaluate, and even to correct— that is, to change rigid, egocentric, repetitive statements into ones that reflect awareness of the other person's ideas.

This activity is not concerned with outcomes. It is immaterial whether a reconciliation is affected or one point of view triumphs over the other or both parties "agree to disagree" or they end up as they began—diametrically opposed to each other's position. *What is germane is that neither speaker be ignored.* If a point is made, it must be recognized and reckoned with, not necessarily accepted.

Take Both Sides

The teacher chooses a topic that lends itself to a debate. It can be at any grade level. An elementary topic might be "Children in school should be allowed to get a drink of water anytime they want" whereas a more advanced one could be "Raising the tax on gasoline is a good way to conserve energy." Present one side of it orally. Discuss it briefly with the class. Then present the other side. When the class gets the idea that a topic can generally have several points of view, make a grab bag of topics—each written on an index card. A pupil selects one and gives his opinion. Choose another pupil to give the opposing view. When they become somewhat adept at this, let the same child take both sides of the argument, first presenting one, then the other. In the beginning, it is advisable to allow some time for writing the "speech"; later, it can be done with just a few brief notes or even extemporaneously. (Spelling and penmanship don't count—as long as the child can "read" it back.)

An interesting extension could be to have the class decide which of the two arguments was presented more effectively by the child. Verbal feedback can be given by the teacher and the class regarding the reasons for their choices. In having his communication strengths and weaknesses analyzed—and in a nonthreatening atmosphere, at that, since he is competing only with himself—he is being directed toward a more convincing rendition in future performances.

The chief purpose of this activity, however, is to demonstrate (and hopefully, the child will internalize) that there is generally more than one side to any given topic. The implication, therefore, is to *really listen to the one with whom you are conversing*— maybe his views have merit and may affect the direction of your argument. At any rate, the fact that you listen to him (whether you agree or not), will render you a more interesting—and interested —communicator.

Dear Abby

Divide the class into pairs. One pupil writes a letter seeking help with some personal problem; the other pupil then writes his advice. (There are some logistical considerations here growing out of the fact that while one pupil is writing, the other will have nothing to do. The teacher can remedy this by encouraging them to write briefly and quickly, structuring the activity so that each child can be occupied productively while his partner is writing, or assigning it as written homework.) These can then be read to the class for further discussion, evaluation, additions, or alternative advice. In launching this activity, the teacher may provide several "problems" and elicit solutions from the class orally. Later, the written format can be introduced. Finally, the teacher can encourage spontaneous discussion—that is, two pupils are selected; one tells his problem, the other gives the solutions. An example follows:

132

Dear Abby,

I love my dog very much but my parents say we can't keep him unless I walk him every morning. The trouble is that I'm too busy in the morning getting dressed and getting my books together so that I can go to school.

John

Dear John,

Try to get your books ready and also lay out your clothes the night before. Perhaps you can go to bed a little earlier so that you can get up a little earlier.

Abby

It is important that each child get considerable experience in asking the questions as well as in offering solutions. The advice seeker can be guided in evaluating the proffered advice; he must *listen* in order to make a sound judgment. Even more so, the adviser must listen, empathize with the other pupil, organize his thoughts, then express them. This activity, then, goes directly toward fostering attention to and interest in others.

The Third Party

Create skits for a cast of three people with the bulk of the conversation to be carried out by two of them, the third person interjecting occasionally. The purpose of this activity is for a given child to get guided experience in conversing with one individual, while not ignoring the third party. Some suggested settings are:

- A teacher is conferring with a parent. The third party is the child.
- A shoe salesperson is talking with a male customer. The third party is his wife.
- A doctor is talking with his nurse. The third party is the patient.
- A waiter is taking a guest's order. The third party is the guest's companion.
- Two baseball fans are arguing at the Yankee Stadium. The third party is another fan in the adjoining seat.
- Two campers are discussing their feelings. (It's the first day of camp.) The third party is another camper.

133

- Two friends are standing in line for a movie and discussing the cast. The third party is a stranger standing next to them in the line.

What Else?

Two pupils are selected to engage in an informal conversation. Initially, it is a good idea to assign the topic; later, they can think of their own. At the end of a prearranged period (two to three minutes), stop the conversation and ask them various questions dealing with their incidental observations: During what part of the talk did Henry speak softest? What did he do when he was excited? When Mary was having difficulty trying to think of the names of TV shows for each night, what part of her face did she touch? At what point in the conversation did Mary continue talking at the same time that Henry spoke?

The players can be instructed to face away from each other before being asked questions such as: What color was Henry's shirt? What was Mary holding in her hand?

Additional pupils can join the cast primarily as listeners. Then the two original players can be questioned regarding their observations of the others: Who sat closest to Mary? Who sat between Tom and Helen? At what point did James stand?

A videotape can be extremely helpful since it can serve to verify the answers. Needless to say, it is important to ask the players questions concerning the conversation itself—that is, what did each person say and what did they learn from one another? If care is not taken to do this, the pupils may become more skillful in *incidental* learning, while missing the point at hand. Clearly, the goal is a blend of the two: The effective, interesting speaker—and learner—concentrates on the words themselves, but does not ignore the nonverbal messages; he pays attention to what the speaker is saying, but simultaneously makes some peripheral observations.

COMMUNICATING WITH ACCURACY

Inaccuracy in communication, when it is not the result of mental or physical handicaps, can arise in many ways. It can reflect a lack of flexibility—for example, inability to deal with words that sound alike or have multiple meanings, continuing to belabor a previous point although a new point is now in order, missing the gist of a cartoon, joke, or social situation, talking all subjects "to the hilt" instead of giving some the cursory attention they deserve. An overly literal individual is often an "inaccurate" communicator because of difficulty in handling idioms, proverbs, metaphors, and the like. Egocentricity can result in a conversation that makes sense only if the listener is privy to some information that, in reality, is the sole province of the speaker. Still another example of inaccuracy in communication results from illogical language and/or thinking processes (for instance, drawing inappropriate conclusions, not asking the right questions, confusing probability for possibility, not differentiating between fact and opinion, not "reading between the lines," not seeing cause-effect relationships). The following activities are designed to foster greater accuracy in communication:

What Do They Mean?

Prepare a brief story (oral and/or written) in which an individual makes a final statement that, from a standpoint of sheer context, is incongruous with the preceding events. It is a case of sarcasm (which, incidentally, may be either complimentary or derogatory). The child must recognize—and be able to formulate —the true feelings of the speaker. Here's an example (Riddle and Wall, 1963, 21):

> As Mary was getting up she was planning all that she was going to do. At breakfast she reported her plans to her parents. Eating quickly she dashed into the yard to plant some seeds. Then she painted her dollhouse. Next, she cleaned her room. Finally it was time for lunch. She was in a hurry to go to the library so she gulped her food.
>
> "Really, Mary," said Mother, "you are a very lazy girl." What Mother really meant was _____

In the beginning, the teacher may elicit from the children the reason for the incongruity; later, the pupil simply writes (or states) the true meaning. A variation might be for the teacher to compose stories of this type omitting the final statement. Give the pupils practice in creating a true ending as well as a sarcastic one.

Probability and Possibility

Write (or state) pairs of events. The children must decide which is more likely to occur. Some examples follow:

a. Mr. Smith gets his paycheck.
b. Mr. Smith finds a twenty-dollar bill.

a. The ice cream melted in the winter.
b. The ice cream melted in the summer.

a. The pupil says, "Please sit down."
b. The teacher says, "Please sit down."

a. A librarian hurts his thumb with a hammer.
b. A carpenter hurts his thumb with a hammer.

a. The new teacher lost her way getting to school.
b. The school bus driver lost his way getting to school.

a. The barber fought with the man.
b. The policeman fought with the man.

Each pupil should, of course, be able to state the reasons for his selection. An extension of this activity is to elicit from the students the circumstances under which the less probable event might occur (for example, a librarian could hurt her thumb with a hammer while hanging a picture on the wall, ice cream could melt indoors in the winter).

Never, Always, or Sometimes

This activity is clearly related to the previous one: That is, even if something occurs very infrequently, it still has a possibility (no matter how remote) of happening. The correct answer in this instance will have to be *sometimes,* rather than the dogmatic—and illogical—*never.*

Some items suggested by Keith (1972, 128–130) are:

1. Trains (never, always, sometimes) run on tracks.
2. Children (never, always, sometimes) grow taller than their parents.
3. A fly is (never, always, sometimes) bigger than an elephant.
4. The sun is (never, always, sometimes) hot.
5. Men (never, always, sometimes) wear neckties.
6. A fish (never, always sometimes) lives in water.
7. A week is (never, always, sometimes) longer than a day.
8. We can (never, always, sometimes) see stars at night.
9. Money is (never, always, sometimes) made of paper.
10. Eyes are (never, always, sometimes) brown.
11. Boats (never, always, sometimes) have sails.

The teacher must be prepared to accept an answer that is somewhat unexpected. Some children are more creative and see more possibilities. For example, a very arduous day can *seem* longer than a week, a porpoise jumping out of water for a few seconds continues to live, and a derailed train (or a train that has stopped) does not run on the tracks. The key is to allow the child to explain the reasons for his answer. If the logic becomes evident, he deserves praise. Truly bizarre answers and "reasoning" should of course tactfully be discouraged.

Yes, No, and Maybe

Present a child with a list of statements (for example, you breathe with your lungs), each to be answered with yes, no, or maybe. Bush and Giles (1977, 49) believe that this activity nurtures attention skills (the child must concentrate in order to arrive at his response) and also provides experience in logical thinking. The latter is facilitated by asking the child to state the reasons for his answer. Among those statements presented by the authors (pp. 49–51) are:

1. Apples are just little red homes for worms.
2. The ball is square.
3. A metal button is shiny.
4. A brick wall is hard.
5. A school bus is heavy.

6. Bananas can telephone.
7. The children went to the ice-cream shop and bought a truck.
8. Bubble gum is not sticky.
9. When a person cries, he is sad.
10. A gallon of water is more than a handful.
11. An air-conditioner makes you feel hot.
12. Black is the opposite of white.
13. Is cheese made to eat?
14. A red light means *go*.

Again, do not automatically rule out a "wrong" answer. Ask the child to state his reason. He might be right in his own way. (For example, if you stand outside a building, the air-conditioner's exhaust does indeed feel hot.)

Fact and Opinion

Present pairs of sentences (written or oral), each pair depicting one fact and one opinion. Some examples are:

Bananas taste better than oranges.
Vanilla is the most popular flavor in the United States.

Smoking cigarettes is harmful to your health.
You catch a cold by breathing in cold air.

Red is a pretty color.
A typewriter is a useful invention.

Abraham Lincoln was president during the Civil War.
High school teachers are smarter than elementary school teachers.

The teacher can provide the class with cues and strategies for differentiating these two types of statements. Some key questions are: Is it possible? Might a reasonably intelligent person disagree? Words like *good, best, better, bad, worse, worst, pretty, ugly, nice, interesting*—all point toward opinion.

Predicaments and Remedies

One child (or team) is instructed to write imaginary predicaments—for example, What would you do if you broke your eyeglasses? What would you do if you lost a library book? What would you do if a waiter spilled chocolate pudding on your white slacks? Another child (or team), without looking at these written predicaments, invents remedies to *their own* problems—for example, I would go on a diet. I would ask for a raise in allowance. I would scream as loud as I could. The teacher arranges the pupils in pairs—one child reads his predicament, the other reads his remedy. The results are often hilarious inasmuch as the answer-writer has no prior knowledge of the question.

In teaching this game to the children, the teacher must first ensure that they understand the nature of the true predicament-remedy situation. In other words, she will at first elicit answers that are appropriate to a stated question. In this way, the child's concept of cause-effect relationships is nourished. In fact, the solution-writers have a much more difficult time than do the predicament-writers: They must conceive of a predicament as well as its remedy, and then discard the predicament prior to writing the remedy, whereas those who compose the questions need only formulate a predicament and write it. In instructing pupils to compose solutions, the teacher may initially give them considerable practice in listing both the problems and their solutions. Gradually, they can be guided in thinking up a predicament, remembering it, and writing its remedy. Since the two roles are different, it is important that all children, via role switching, gain experience in both.

After the class learns how to play this game, the teacher can ask them to discuss why they consider certain matchings funny. In order to appreciate the humorous (which is often unexpected or even absurd), one must be aware of the anticipated, the general, the logical.

Twenty Questions

One pupil (or team) decides upon an object. The other player (or team) tries to unearth its identity by asking questions to which they will receive only yes-no answers. The aim is to guess the object within twenty questions. Research (Moshner and Hornsby, 1966, 90–93) has shown that use of logical strategy—specifically, questions that narrow the total array of possibilities—is a function of age. Suppose the object is a bed. The experienced player might ask, "Is it usually found inside a house?" then, "Is it furniture?" and so on, whereas the less mature player begins immediately by guessing specific objects. It was found that six-year-olds simply guess at answers, whereas eleven-year-olds ask a considerable number of strategic questions. One clear advantage of the more mature strategy is that even a no answer is useful. (A no to "Is it bigger than a breadbox?" says, in fact, that it is smaller than a breadbox.) A no answer to the guessing approach is hardly helpful since the remaining array still totals infinity minus one!

This game can be played by substituting problems for objects (Moshner and Hornsby, 1966, 87), for example, "A man was driving down the road in his car, the car went off the road and hit a tree. Find out what happened." The researchers (p. 88) contrast the strategic question, "Did it have anything to do with the weather?" with the wild guess, "Did the driver get stung in the eye by a bee and lose control . . . ?"

The guesser is seen as an impulsive individual. His approach lacks logic. If it is a group game, and he continues to guess, ignoring the hints generated by his teammates' strategic questions, then his teammates will find him boring, disinterested, and egocentric. Experience in playing this game (and others like it—such as, "What's My Line?") and instruction in utilizing the more mature, collaborative strategy might help develop a more interesting, more sociocentric, and in a sense, a more accurate conversationalist.

Bit by Bit

Select a cartoon: for example, a picture that shows a girl having lunch with her mother in a restaurant. There are three place settings. They are sitting under a window and looking out. Father is outside near his parked car, pleading with a police officer not to give him a ticket. The caption reads, "If daddy has to go to jail, can I have his dessert?" Divide this cartoon into a series of transparent overlays, calling the pupil's attention to the various elements as they are added. Thus he is guided in seeing the important ingredients one set at a time and will be more likely to get the gist of the joke. Select other cartoons and gradually reduce the number of transparencies.

This can be done with verbal jokes as well by initially presenting each point slowly, calling the pupil's attention to it, and reviewing all previous points as each new one is stated. Gradually make the points longer and fade out the review.

Do You Know What I Mean?

Prepare a series of brief monologues, some of which will "make sense" only if the listener is familiar with the speaker's topic: After all, if I greet you with "I ran into Carol Anderson," it presumes that you know who Carol Anderson is. Other examples will be more general in nature, and do not require any specialized knowledge.

An example of a generalized monologue follows:

Hi, Jim. It sure is cold outside. I think I'll get home right away because it might snow. I'll have to shovel the snow from my walk because my dad hurt his back and won't be able to.

A specialized one would be:

Hello, Margaret. My car sure has been giving me trouble lately. The brake shoes are worn down. I wish I had realized that before because now the rivets are exposed and scratched the drums. They need refacing and that will cost more money.

Guide the children in determining whether or not a given statement has a strong potential for being understood by the average listener. Teaching activities could include deciding what the listener has to know in advance in order to comprehend a particular statement, deciding upon the reasonableness of the assumption that most people would have that knowledge, separating "general" from "specialized" statements that have been written on index cards, rewriting "specialized" statements into "general" ones, listing each pupil's hobbies and interests and taking a class poll to see the frequency with which each is shared.

Also, it is advisable to set up guidelines regarding the use of "specialized" statements: The speaker could ask the listener in advance if he is familiar with the topic and/or if he is interested in it, or the speaker could explain some specialized topic or relationship so that it now can be comprehended by the listener.

141

Please Stop!

Prepare several scripts, each entailing two characters. One asks the other a lead-in question (for example, Did you enjoy your vacation? Do you like your new job? How is your brother getting along? Do you get a lot of homework?). The second then answers the question. Sometimes the answer is of the appropriate length, but in other cases, it goes on and on and on.

Suppose Mother asks Helen if she enjoyed the "Sweet Sixteen Party," and Helen responds, "Yes. It got off to a slow start because the early arrivers were all too quiet and shy. But later, Michael and his friends came in. They're real lively and a lot of fun, and soon everybody was having a great time." This seems to be just about the correct quantity of verbalization. Assuming Mother is genuinely interested, a lone yes or no is too perfunctory. (It is not unlike the comic routine—"Do you know what time it is?" "Yes.")

On the other hand, Helen didn't overwhelm her mother with a barrage of details:

> Oh, yes. It was supposed to start at eight-thirty. I arrived at eight-fifteen. I talked a little bit to Joan's mother. Then I had to use the bathroom. Afterward, I couldn't unlock the door. I banged real hard and Mrs. White let me out. Three boys came in. They were dogs. Not really, one was even a little cute. We had strawberry ice cream. I spilled a little on my dress, but some cold water got most of it out. There was some real great music, but it was a little too loud. etc., etc., etc.

The teacher can present the class with scripts arranged in pairs, each containing one appropriate and one inappropriate example. These may be either in written or oral form. Tape recordings can be useful. The class can receive sequential instruction in distinguishing the acceptable sample from the unacceptable one. Guidelines can be drawn up regarding the customary length and degree of detail for any specific script sequence. Later, the children can receive practice in composing such scripts and in correcting—that is, rewriting—those portions deemed inappropriate.

Same Word—Different Meaning

Our language abounds with words whose meaning changes depending upon their context. The overly concrete child can be perplexed by these. Idioms ("It's raining cats and dogs"), metaphors (an ironclad rule), and proverbs ("Look before you leap") are not to be taken literally. Similar confusion results from homonyms (flour—flower), homographs or multiple-meaning words (the *top* of the desk, I spin my *top*), and heteronyms or words that are spelled the same but have different pronunciations (I *wind* my watch, the *wind* is blowing).

A total language program is necessary to increase the individual's prowess for dealing with these kinds of words. Activities would include vocabulary building; practice in spelling; decoding words phonetically, and especially, in using context clues to discover the meanings of words and expressions; auditory training; composing a sentence using a given word; matching proverbs with their referent stories; and explaining and composing metaphors. Certainly, an exposure to literature and drama is a major factor. Above all, the individual must develop confidence in his ability to comprehend what he reads and what he hears, so that if a word, phrase, or sentence doesn't "make sense," he does not attribute it to his own inadequacy; rather, he asks "Is it a new word?" "a new usage?" "a novel expression?"

Give Me a Ring

The teacher dramatizes an incorrect way to use a telephone. A real phone (disconnected), or even a toy one—as opposed to an imaginary one—is necessary in order to enable the pupils to see the specific source of error. The pupils try to guess what is wrong. In a game format, the successful guesser can become the next performer. Some of the portrayed errors might be:

1. Standing at the phone, saying "We've talked only an hour. I have plenty of time."
2. Whispering into the phone.
3. Talking too loudly into the phone.
4. Slamming down the receiver.

5. Putting the phone in its cradle sideways.
6. Dialing with the receiver in the cradle.
7. Saying "I'm not getting any dial tone," then dialing anyway.
8. Chewing food while speaking.
9. Leaving the phone off the hook and walking away.
10. Saying "Oh, I must dial the operator and tell her about the accident I saw," then dialing the letter *O* from *MNO*.
11. Dialing without bringing one's finger all the way to the finger stop.
12. Talking on the phone, then suddenly beginning to talk to someone else in the room without covering the receiver.
13. Talking on the phone but using a lot of gestures (for example, shrugging shoulders, nodding head) instead of words.
14. Talking with one's mouth too close to the speaker.
15. Talking with one's mouth too far from the speaker.
16. Talking into the receiver instead of the speaker.

Draw What I Say

The teacher prepares several charts, each having a simplified drawing: a house, a skyscraper, some trees, a sailboat. She selects one of them and calls on a pupil. He is not allowed to look at the drawing, but attempts to duplicate it at the chalkboard by following instructions from the members of the class: for example, "Start at the top at about the middle and draw a straight line going down." The class can be paired off, one person drawing and the other instructing. The child describing the picture is permitted to use gestures (for example, denoting "very little," "large," "keep going") along with verbal language. Roles should be reversed frequently so that each child gets experience in giving directions as well as in following them. Granted that this activity, essentially, deals with a somewhat discrete range of language and perception involving spatial orientation, direction, and distance, it does nourish attention and listening skills, discourages impulsivity, and offers experience in receiving and expressing some nonverbal messages such as "You're right on target," "not quite," "no, that's all wrong."

COMMUNICATING WITH EXPRESSION

If you communicate without expression, you are perceived as an uninteresting person. You are also judged to be shallow emotionally since you don't speak with *feeling*. Finally, much of your message will fail to get across if you leave out the nonverbal elements of conversation.

In some cases, the child who does not communicate with expression adequately may have a specific motor problem: That is, he perceives the proper gesture for "come here," "I don't know," and "so-so," the eye movement signifying boredom, incredulity, and sadness, and the facial expressions of surprise, enthusiasm, and disgust, but he cannot duplicate them. He may need special instructions in body movement (including eye movement and facial expression). Just as he learns a dance step, he may learn how to shrug his shoulders.

In other instances, motor coordination may be intact, but perceptual deficits may be present. If visual imperception causes a child difficulty in distinguishing a circle from an oval, he may also experience difficulty in differentiating a smile from a smirk. Similarly, the child with auditory perception deficit who cannot distinguish between "bad" and "bed," "hospital" and "hop-si-tal," a low-pitched note from a high-pitched one, may be equally inept in discerning the tone of sarcasm, the rising inflection of surprise, or the gradually elevated pitch coupled with staccato delivery denoting mounting anger.

If the teacher realizes that a child has a motor problem primarily, then the nonverbal communication training activities can emphasize expression (that is, talking, gesturing, pantomiming). If perceptual impairment is at the root of the lonely child's nonverbal communication deficit, then he should get lots of instruction and practice in reception (listening to the speaker and watching his movements). One is not exclusive of the other. The vast majority of the activities in this book entail reversible roles—that is, one pupil sends messages while another receives them; positions can be switched. The following activities are suggested for nurturing communication with expression:

145

How Did I Say It?

Show the class that the same words can often be said in a variety of ways, each denoting a different feeling. Begin with the expression *Oh! Yeah!* This can be said in the following manner:

1. angry, challenging
     (Oh, yeah, what are you going to do about it?)
2. disgusted
     (Oh, yeah, knowing you, I didn't expect any better.)
3. happy, enthusiastic
     (Would you like some ice cream? Oh, yeah!)
4. fright
     (It's getting dark and we don't have a flashlight. Oh, yeah.)
5. boredom
     (His speech will take at least forty-five minutes more. Oh, yeah.)
6. pride
     (Did the class elect you president? Oh, yeah.)
7. nervousness, confirming an inner thought
     (I want to go to the movies, and, oh yeah, then I have to go to the, oh yeah, hardware store.)

At first, use only two possibilities (say, anger and pride). Let the children take turns performing and interpreting. Later, introduce additional portrayals. Children can be paired: One performs while the other tries to determine the expression being characterized; then the roles can be reversed.

A variation of this game can be to prepare an index card for each member of the class. On each card is written an emotion—pride, boredom, etc. These are equally divided: For example, in a class of twenty-four pupils, there may be four "disgusts," four "frights," four "happys," and so on. The children can walk around the room, saying "Oh, yeah" to one another, each in the manner written on his index card. The object of this game is for the pupils to find their partners.

Later, other words can be introduced (never, thanks, wait, remember). Gradually, this program can progress to sentences (for instance, I don't know, I'll do it). Hennings (1974, 166–167) suggests a prepared handout sheet listing the words as well as the

146

manner in which they are to be enacted. One child can then choose a word and the manner of dramatization. The rest of the class tries to guess the emotion being portrayed. The first one who is correct becomes the next actor.

One of the handout sheets recommended by Hennings is as follows:

I. Ways of speaking a word or sentence:

with sadness	with determination
with regret	with concern
with fear	with lack of concern
with happiness	with enthusiasm
with pride	with vengeance
with disgust	with surprise
with anticipation	with sarcasm

II. Words to speak:

please	often	when	crazy
never	sorry	how	come
good	help	where	no
me	oh	next	yes
you	why	now	stop

The astute teacher will modify this activity depending upon the maturity, age, interest, prior experience, and skill of the pupils. Some of the variables that he can manipulate are the number of items used in any one set, vocabulary, language complexity, wording of the instructions, and the number of samples ("test-runs") prior to the game.

It is possible to prepare a brief scenario involving two (or more) people. The identical script is used for a series of different settings, but the tones of voices, facial expressions, and body language cues will vary in accordance to the emotional context of each specific situation. Polak (1976, 2) suggests the following:

Lemon Drop

A. Hi.
B. Hi.
A. How are you?

147

B. Fine, and you?

A. OK. Would you like a lemon drop?

B. Sure.

A. Here.

B. Thanks. Well, I have to be going now.

A. Bye.

B. Bye.

Suggested situations:
    two joggers
    two drunks
    two spies
    two tightrope artists
    two lovers
    two old friends
    two children waiting outside the principal's office, etc.

Magic Wand

Let one pupil begin reciting—reading a brief script, a poem, a story (or part of a story) from his reader. At the onset, he is handed an index card on which is written an adverb (angrily, sadly, nervously) and he must perform in that manner. After a little while, the teacher touches him with a magic wand—a pointer or a yardstick on whose tip is affixed another index card listing a different adverb. Upon reading (silently) the new adverb, the pupil continues reciting, but changes his manner of delivery accordingly.

The rest of the class must guess the adverb. Instead of shouting out their answers (and in doing so, interrupting the performer), they can write their answers, previously having numbered their papers to coincide with the number of different adverbs the teacher had planned for any given performer.

In some instances (for poor readers, for example) the pupil may recite from memory. The selections can range in complexity from such items as nursery rhymes and "Twinkle Twinkle Little Star" to the Gettysburg Address. (Clearly, the shorter pieces will have to be recited several times.) For variation, the teacher may ask a pupil simply to count from one to one hundred or to recite the alphabet, but to feign the various feelings suggested by each

148

touch of the magic wand. Initially, the pool of adverbs for any given set should be listed on the chalkboard in random order. This will render the activity less "open-ended" and eliminate any possible spelling problems.

This activity is particularly worthwhile in that its chief characteristic is change. And one ingredient of effective expression is also change—change in tempo, in pitch, in volume, a rising inflection, a movement toward (or away from) the listener, a sudden pause, and so forth. It is not accidental that the word *monotonous* (with its prefix *mono* indicating *one* or *sameness*) means *boring*.

Format for Feeling

Give a work sheet to each child. Each sheet will tell of a specific occurrence designed to evoke strong feelings in school age children. Some examples are:

> You move into a new neighborhood. You are lonely. You see a group of children and feel certain that they will be unfriendly. You approach them timidly. One of them is in your class and is very happy to see you. All the children welcome you.

> It's June. You realize that you are doing poorly in school, and that you will have to study harder next term. But you know at least three classmates who are worse students than you. The teacher gives out the report cards. You are the only one left back.

> You have a job as a newsboy (girl) after school. You like it fine and are beginning to save your money for a new bicycle. Besides the money, you like the idea of responsibility and the praise from many of your satisfied customers. The boss tells you that you can't have the job anymore because he promised to give it to his nephew.

At first, a word-selection box is prepared for the children from which to choose answers to a series of open-ended questions like this:

```
a. I feel very _____
b. I feel that I'd like to _____
   _____
c. It's just like _____
```

The answers are all words of feeling. For example, the answers to the "newspaper delivery" story could be: (a) sad, disappointed, angry, furious, miserable, hurt; (b) go home and cry, scream at him (her), give him (her) a punch, break something; (c) being stabbed in the back, being treated like a dog, a sad movie. This pool of answers should be displayed on a chart throughout.

After one or two experiences using word-box choices, the children might give their own feeling words in answers to similar selections. Then each pupil recites his feeling card. The class discusses the appropriateness of the words and the effectiveness of the nonverbal communication. True, this approach to expressions of feeling may lead to a somewhat stilted, superficial, or stereotyped concept of what emotions are about. After all, the way one feels is a highly individual matter, whereas this activity treats all the pupils' expressions of emotion in a very uniform manner. (That is, we do not express our emotions consistently with the actual words: "I feel——," "I feel like I'd like to ——," "It's just like——.") However, its high degree of structure makes it a most helpful teaching tool if used judiciously—namely, if utilized only until the child gains confidence and more experience in expressing his emotions in a variety of ways.

Are You Convincing?

One person often attempts to persuade another: a child pleads with his mother for an extension of the bedtime hour, the high school student exhorts the guidance counselor (or dean) to change his program, a used-car dealer cajoles the prospective customer, an overanxious parent coaxes—gently but persistently—a shy child to go out and "make friends." As he becomes engrossed in his argument, he pleads, not only with words, but with eye movement, facial expression, gestures, posture, and tone of voice. Feedback becomes very important as he attempts to evaluate the impact he is having upon the other person; he then modifies his performance based upon this data.

The classroom teacher can select two pupils to enact a given scenario. Among the situations suggested by Hennings (p. 151) are:

Convince a salesperson to let you return a nonreturnable item.

Convince someone to buy a product you are selling.

Convince someone to give up smoking.

Convince someone to go to a horror movie with you—he doesn't like horror movies.

Convince your mother or father that you need a new coat (dress, shirt, shoes).

Convince a friend to drive slowly to conserve gasoline.

Convince a teacher that you shouldn't have so much homework.

The teacher may wish to write scripts (or partial scripts) at first to accommodate overly shy, self-conscious pupils. As soon as possible, they should be encouraged to create their own extemporaneously. Spontaneous dialogues foster ingenuity, imagination, and a sense of humor. An anecdote by Art Buchwald published in *Reader's Digest* (May 1977, p. 129) is a good example of this:

> The fledgling actors were told to imagine that it was World War II, and the last plane to leave the Philippines was about to take off. They had to try to persuade guards to let them on the overloaded plane.
>
> Each student made a passionate plea—one said that she was pregnant, another that he had to report to the president. All their pleas failed. Finally, one student actor ran up to the guards and screamed, "I have to get on the plane! I just have to get on the plane!"
>
> "Why?" asked the guard.
>
> "I'm the pilot!"

Puppets

Many of the activities described in this chapter (and, to a lesser extent, in the previous one) lend themselves handily to the medium of puppets. In general, these should be of the simple, "hand-puppet" variety.

Puppets can be used to stimulate children to participate in skits (or in individual performances). Providing children with this novel experience heightens their attention and motivation. It also nourishes spontaneity and creativity. In addition, since no puppet

151

—even those of the professional puppeteer—can perform the vast array of body movements, gestures, and facial expressions that are part of human communication, the child using this vehicle almost always tries (even at the subconscious level) to interject more vocal expression. Above all, puppets are recommended for the shy, withdrawn, self-conscious child. He receives the accolades of the performer, yet the audience is not scrutinizing *him,* they are looking at the *puppet.*

THE TEACHER IS THE KEY

Merely going through the various games and exercises cited in this and the previous chapter does not ensure success. In fact, at bottom, such activities merely *test* the pupil in those social skills in which he is deficient. Instead of being a *learning* experience for the lonely, socially ineffective and imperceptive child, they may actually become still another source of *failure* for him.

The principal factor is the teacher. She must know the child—his likes and dislikes, his weaknesses and strengths, his learning style. She must be aware of his affective needs as well as his cognitive ones. She must recognize his limitations. Since many of the activities place the child "in the spotlight," the teacher must assiduously avoid embarrassing, humiliating and/or dehumanizing him. (Judicious use of role reversal in which the child observes rather than performs is essential.) The teacher, herself, must become expert in nonverbal communication so that she can be aware of the signals she is emitting and will be better able to "read" the child.

Her expertise as a teacher is critical. She must be able to proceed sequentially (from the simpler to the complex, from shorter activities to longer ones, from using "neutral themes" to more emotionally laden ones). She must be able to structure the lesson for success. She must be an effective leader (although a low-keyed one, in many instances). She must be thoroughly familiar with the activities, materials, and programs. She must know how to teach diagnostically: For example, if a child doesn't pantomime "I don't know" (shrugging of shoulders) correctly, she must be able to probe further in order to determine whether it is an expressive problem, a receptive problem or both.

Just as the child's ultimate success in social perception is a function of the quality of education he receives, so is the teacher's effectiveness dependent upon the preparation she undergoes. Teacher-training institutions should design courses that stress the teaching of social-recreational skills. Gym teachers and English (especially drama) teachers should receive training in making modifications for the less able student. Courses at the college level dealing specifically with nonverbal communication and social perception should become an integral part of the education major's overall preparation.

REFERENCES

Bush, Wilma Jo, and Giles, Marion T. *Aids to Psycholinguistic Teaching.* 2nd ed. Columbus, Ohio: Charles E. Merrill Co., 1977.

Furth, Hans G., and Wachs, Harry. *Thinking Goes to School: Piaget's Theory in Practice.* New York: Oxford University Press, 1975.

Hennings, Dorothy Grant. *Smiles, Nods, and Pauses.* New York: Citation Press, 1974.

Keith, Robert L. *Speech and Language Rehabilitation: A Workbook for the Neurologically Impaired.* Danville, Ill.: The Interstate Printers and Publishers, Inc., 1972.

Moshner, Frederic A., and Hornsby, Joan Rigney. "On Asking Questions." In Jerome S. Bruner *et al.,* eds., *Studies in Cognitive Growth.* New York: John Wiley and Sons, Inc., 1966, pp. 86–102.

Polak, Eddy. *Teacher's Aid.* Montreal: Quebec Association for Children with Learning Disabilities, 1976.

Reader's Digest, May 1977.

Riddle, Evelyn, and Wall, Kathleen. *Reading Adventures, Grade 4—First Half.* St. Louis, Mo.: Milliken Publishing Co, 1963.

CHAPTER 11

Perspectives

For years, behavioral scientists and educational psychologists have guided teachers toward a more clinical approach. They point out that by means of diagnostic-prescription teaching coupled with behavior-modification techniques, it is now possible to "train" the pupil to perform any number of feats—including the achievement of acceptable nonverbal communication skills. And, in fact, a guiding principle of this book has been that social perception (and nonverbal communication abilities), for the most part, are learned behaviors and therefore amenable to teaching. However, as any student of task analysis knows, the observable behavioral objective that is specified is seldom the *real* purpose of the lesson. Following instruction, we can see the pupil's terminal behavior, but we cannot witness his cognitive processes in operation nor can we gauge the degree of emotional significance that this learning experience holds for him. (To put it differently, we observe what he *does,* but can only surmise what he *thinks* and how he *feels.*) In addition, we notice what the student *can* do, but are given no inkling of what he *will* do. We can teach a pupil to read signs of anger in another, but we don't know whether or not he will use this data productively. We can teach a child how to differentiate between a logical statement and an illogical one, but in informal spontaneous situations he may continue to speak illogically. We may teach a child how to gesture "I'm disgusted with you," but he may still lack the temerity to express this feeling. We can teach a child to recognize—and to make—a happy face, but he may still be sad. He may learn how to identify sarcasm, yet continue to invite it.

Lessons in social perception should never be approached as purely behavioral and/or cognitive experiences; the affective domain must permeate every facet of the teaching-learning experience. The *true* goal of strengthening social perception in the lonely child—namely to render him more acceptable to others *and to himself*—dictates that he must learn *affectively:* He must *feel* it, not just *know* it. He must not accept the perceptions and learnings of others, but must develop his own.

The teacher (or parent) must understand the lonely child, his history of past hurts, his vulnerability. Good mental hygiene practices are imperative. Central to any contemplated program of nonverbal communication remediation is the realization that this child is probably extremely self-conscious. Yet, in many of the instructional activities suggested in this book (and elsewhere), the child is "on display." Therefore, the teacher must patently avoid scolding, complaining, or criticizing. Even a minimal performance should receive abundant—but specific and sincere—praise; that is, "thimbleful" of growth must be recognized and acknowledged.

The instruction should be structured for success. It is a good idea to start well below the level of the child and gradually build up to more difficult activities. The child should never be coerced into performing, but encouraged to be a spectator until he feels more comfortable performing. Overlearning should be stressed in deference to the adage "practice makes perfect." The lonely, socially imperceptive child usually has more than one nonverbal communication "fault." These should be approached with a great deal of sensitivity, intermingled with areas of strength, and certainly, only one at a time—otherwise the instruction will be tantamount to nagging.

Throughout our book, we stressed that the lonely child needs to develop more interest in—*and empathy with*—others. There is another side of the coin: Teachers (and parents) ought to become more empathic toward him. We can help him only if we truly understand him. We have to develop a special insight into his predicament and we must constantly remind ourselves how difficult nonverbal communication really is: We want him to learn how to pay attention to nonverbal communication signals, but at that very moment, he must also listen to the words themselves. He has to attend to what is being said, yet, at the same time, formulate what he is going to say. We want him to concentrate on the one with whom he is speaking, but to be receptive to the peripheral third party as well. Finally, we want him to learn to express emotions, and then we have the effrontery to tell him to *mask* these feelings!

In order to reduce anxiety, the lessons ought to be made as enjoyable as possible. The teacher should approach the instruction with some degree of seriousness ("This is important," "It will help us a lot if we learn how to do these things")—this can minimize any tendency toward giddiness or "horsing around." At the same time, she should not suppress the "fun" aspect inherent in most of these activities and should join in the fun. The teacher's enthusiasm, creativity, relaxed manner, and sheer enjoyment may well prove contagious.

There is a direct tie-in between nonverbal communication training and school guidance programs. "How does one look when angry" is a step away from understanding what *causes* anger, other's reactions to our display of it, and ways for dealing with our angry feelings and with the anger of others directed toward us. Ancillary school personnel (guidance counselors, speech therapists, psychologists) can be utilized for group teaching as well as for individual clinical work. The lonely, socially imperceptive child needs this intervention *remedially* and, if he has concomitant emotional problems, *therapeutically*.

The lonely child, inept in nonverbal communication, riddled with anxiety, frustration, and repressed hostility, and plagued with feelings of self-doubt and self-reproach, may well require psychotherapy (or counseling)—either in conjunction with or as a prerequisite to instruction in nonverbal communication skills. (A total program might include parent counseling, too, inasmuch as the child's image of himself is intimately linked with his parents' feelings about—and reactions to—him.) All of us who endeavor to help the lonely, socially imperceptive child must develop a positive outlook. We must remember two salient points: (1) *In most instances, the child has the mentality and the motivation to improve,* and (2) *the means for improvement ("know-how," programs, materials, resources) are available.* The child must believe —and we must vigorously endeavor to convey this message to him—that he *can* make it. Philosopher Eric Hoffer has told us: It is not the completely downtrodden who seek change, but rather those who feel that change is possible.

The lonely child *can* be helped.

Recommended Sources of Remediation

All the items listed here focus directly upon the remediation of nonverbal communication and social perception deficits as well as upon the minimizing of loneliness. Writings that deal only in research and theory regarding the subjects of nonverbal communication and loneliness were not included inasmuch as many of them have already been cited in other chapters and are listed in the Bibliography.

Teaching materials augment the teacher's efforts: They make the lessons more interesting, they can increase motivation, they can serve to enlarge or modify the instructional syllabus, they can suggest new directions in course contents of social studies and language arts. But the key ingredient in the child's educational growth remains the teacher. In short, teaching materials facilitate learning, but in no way guarantee it.

Parents, also, may use many of these aids with their children. This is an important consideration since the parents' efforts can reinforce those of the teacher and lend more continuity to the training program. Parents of preschool children have an especially important role to play in improving their child's social perception.

(A few activities require the child to verbalize deep-seated, personal feelings. Since the parent and child are so emotionally involved with one another, it may be a good idea for parents to omit these and to utilize those activities in which they feel more comfortable. If in doubt, seek the advice of a professional who knows you and the child.)

TEXTS

Bush, Wilma Jo, and Giles, Marion T. *Aids to Psycholinguistic Teaching. 2nd ed.* Columbus, Ohio: Charles E. Merrill Co., 1977. The activities are based upon the model of the Illinois Test for Psycholinguistic Abilities. The auditory and visual training sections are subdivided into the areas of reception, association, closure, and memory. The chapter concerning verbal expression and manual expression is particularly helpful in the remediation of nonverbal communication skills. Perceptual-motor activities are also listed. The final chapter enumerates some overall guidelines for teachers. The activities are arranged in the order of grade level, ranging from kindergarten to grade eight.

Cedoline, Anthony J. *The Effect of Affect.* San Rafael, Calif.: Academic Therapy Publications, 1977. This book describes over one hundred classroom activities designed to help children develop better relationships, self-esteem, and decision making. The opening chapters, "Love as Cause and Effect," "Love and Respect," and "Tips for Teachers," set the tone for the book, establishing guidelines whereby teachers can recognize the affectively healthy child and stipulating specific teaching attitudes and classroom experiences that can nurture greater emotion in children. Other sections, for example, "Getting to Know You," "Getting to Know More About You," and "Role Playing" foster social interaction, empathy, expression of feeling, imagination, interpreting and expressing body language signals.

Chappel, Bernice M. *Listening and Learning: Practical Activities for Developing Listening Skills, Grades K–3.* Belmont, Calif.: Fearon Publishers, 1973. The book is divided into three sections:

Activities and Games, Poems and Rhymes, Stories and Storytelling. There are seventy-six activities portrayed, many of them designed to foster empathy, logical thinking, imagination, and social interaction. The poems and stories can be used for training in communicating with expression.

Furth, Hans G., and Wachs, Harry. *Thinking Goes to School: Piaget's Theory in Practice.* New York: Oxford University Press, 1975. In applying Piaget's theories to educational practices, the authors have compiled 179 teaching activities, games, and puzzles, which they call "thinking games." The activities are listed in developmental progression: general movement thinking, discriminative movement thinking, visual thinking, auditory thinking, hand thinking (for example, tactual discrimination games), graphic thinking (namely, tracking activities whereby vision guides and directs movements), logical thinking games, and social thinking. The activities under logical thinking can help train children to communicate with greater accuracy, and the social thinking games can enhance social perception skills.

Hennings, Dorothy Grant. *Smiles, Nods, and Pauses.* New York: Citation Press, 1974. This book goes to the heart of nonverbal communication. It covers activities and games that can help children learn to express and to interpret nonverbal messages. Precise instructions are given to the teacher. There are separate sections for pantomiming; engaging in plays and role playing; telling stories and reciting poems; conversing; and listening. The author emphasizes the communication of feelings throughout. Many sources of pertinent children's literature are cited over the course of this book, and an annotated bibliography of additional materials is furnished.

Kirk, Samuel A., and Kirk, Winifred D. *Psycholinguistic Learning Disabilities: Diagnosis and Remediation.* Chicago: University of Illinois Press, 1973. The first portion of this book deals with interpreting performance scores on the Illinois Test for Psycholinguistic Abilities and for diagnosing and analyzing psycholinguistic deficits. The last two chapters cover remediation.

Particularly appropriate are those teaching activities concerned with manual/motor expression and visual reception. Other activities facilitate the development of creative thinking, logical thinking, incidental learning (making peripheral and/or background observations), and attention.

New York City Board of Education, Division of Educational Planning and Support, *Oral Communication: Grades K–6.* Curriculum Bulletin, 1976–1977 Series, No. 2. This bulletin covers the entire range of human communication, including articulation and listening skills. It emphasizes, however, nonverbal communication and social perception—particularly in the sections on "Voice," "Pantomime," "Theater Games," "Creative Dramatics," "Storytelling," and "Social Interaction and Usage." Each chapter is divided into a series of lessons (called guides). Each guide sticks with the well-known lesson plan format: aims, materials, motivation and procedure, culminating activities, follow-up activities. Many useful illustrations and references appear throughout. A bibliography of films and filmstrips, recordings, curriculum bulletins, texts, storybooks, and folklore is included.

Polak, Eddy. *Teacher's Aid.* Montreal: Quebec Association for Children wtih Learning Disabilities, 1976. This book consists of a series of activities designed to help teachers nurture children's creativity, imagination, logical thinking, sense of humor, and self-esteem. A large proportion of the activities and games specifically include pantomiming, communicating with feeling, and the overall reception and expression of nonverbal communication signals. Many of the activities are aimed at the secondary student (or for bright elementary grade children), but these can be scaled down to accommodate the younger, less mature, socially imperceptive pupil.

Russell, David H., and Russell, Elizabeth F. *Listening Aids Through the Grades.* New York: Teachers College Press, Columbia University, 1973. The authors describe 190 activities—some of them for *listening* (that is, perception of sounds and words) and others for *auding* (listening to spoken language with comprehension). The book is divided on the basis of grade level: a main section is for the kindergarten and primary grades and the other for the intermediate grades. Many of the activities involve social interaction and offer training in conversing with greater accuracy, interest, and feeling.

Wiig, Elisabeth H., and Semel, Eleanor Messing. *Language Disabilities in Children and Adolescents.* Columbus, Ohio: Charles E. Merrill Co., 1976. This is an in-depth and comprehensive approach to language disabilities, including assessment and remediation. The specific suggestions for remediating linguistic and perceptual processing deficits and language production deficits nurture more mature, effective, and accurate conversational abilities. The last chapter deals with social perception and includes some excellent activities designed to remediate nonverbal communication problems.

TEXTS (JUVENILE)

Brenner, Barbara. *Faces.* Photographs by George Ancona. New York: E. P. Dutton, 1970. This is a good source for introducing children to facial details and for serving as a springboard into experiences involving facial expressions. Close-up photographs of eyes, lips, a nose, a mouth, and an ear are shown. Also included are pictures of a yawn, a smile, a distasteful expression (in response to a bad odor), a child whispering a secret to another. The text is written on about the second-grade reading level and emphasizes that a given facial element has a variety of functions—for example, a mouth is for talking, eating, laughing, kissing, whistling, and for playing a sousaphone!

Gwynne, Fred. *The King Who Rained.* New York: Young Readers Press, Inc., 1973. The comic drawings in this book illustrate the humor that can abound if one makes an error in the use of homonyms (for example, a picture of a king floating above the ground with rain dripping from him—rain: reign) or in homographs, multiple meaning words (for example, a picture of Mother lying on the top of two spaced chairs, spanning or *bridging* them, the caption reading, "Mommy says not to bother her when she's playing bridge").

Parish, Peggy. *Amelia Bedelia.* Drawings by Fritz Seibel. New York: Scholastic Book Services, 1963. This is a humorous story about Amelia Bedelia, a maid, on her first day of work for the Rogers family. The crux of her problem is that she derives unusual meanings from her list of written instructions. Dust the furniture: She sprinkles dusting powder all over the furniture. Put the lights out: She removes all the bulbs and hangs them on the clothesline. Change the towels: She gets a pair of scissors and cuts designs in the towels (thus changing them). Hence this book can be useful in teaching one not to be overly literal and it also suggests that messages given should be more specific and avoid ambiguities. Additional Amelia Bedelia books include: *Thank You, Amelia Bedelia; Play Ball, Amelia Bedelia;* and *Amelia Bedelia and the Surprise Shower.*

Shwarzrock, Shirley, and Wrenn, C. Gilbert. *The Coping with Series.* Circle Pines, Minnesota: American Guidance Service, Inc., 1973. This series of twenty-three short books is geared to the junior high and high school pupil. They can be used individually (as "free" reading material or as supplementary reading to a guidance or counseling session) or in group instruction. The titles especially appropriate for our concerns are: *Living with Loneliness; Can You Talk with Someone Else?; You Always Communicate Something; Do I Know the "Me" Others See?; To Like and Be Liked.* A teacher's manual containing suggested procedures for instruction is included.

The Silver Burdett Social Studies Series (Morristown, N.J., 1976) was designed to be used in teaching social studies in the elementary and junior high schools. These books are especially recommended because both the pictures and the text are highly effective in evoking discussion of feelings and attitudes. (For example, one exercise shows photographs of two world leaders orating; the student is asked to determine the speakers' feelings.)

Another feature of this series is that it frequently elicits the individual pupil's opinion, implying that his ideas are worthwhile and important; hence it heightens self-esteem.

All the texts are basically oriented toward *people* and their social interaction rather than just places, isolated historical facts, and various geographic phenomena. In fact, almost all the pictures in each book portray people as an integral part of whatever social studies concept is under consideration. It is not surprising that each title in the series contains the word *people*—for example, "People in Regions" and "People and Ideas."

The texts come with problem-solving work sheets, spirit master activity sheets, sound-filmstrips, and individualized learning packages (for slow learners).

WORKBOOKS

Boning, Richard A. *Supportive Reading Skills Series.* Baldwin, N.Y.: Dexter and Westbrook, Ltd., 1975. This series is comprised of twelve different titles. The following ones can be useful in helping pupils speak with greater accuracy: *Reading Homonyms, Reading Homographs* (the same word having totally unrelated meanings: I look *like* you. I *like* to play), *Mastering Multiple Meanings* (the same word with somewhat related meanings: My cat is lost! I *miss* her. We will *miss* the bus), and *Reading Heteronyms* (different words with identical spelling: I *wind* my watch. The *wind* is blowing). Each title comes in a set of workbooks according to grade level: *Reading Homonyms* ranges from grades one through nine; *Reading Homographs*—one through five; *Mastering Multiple Meanings*—grades one and two; and *Reading Heteronyms*—grades three through five. The workbooks are attractive. Each page is humorously illustrated, thus lending itself very handily to such activities as pantomiming and dramatization. Also provided are a teacher's manual, pretests and posttests, and spirit masters for duplicating the work sheets (on which the pupil writes his answers).

The Milliken Series (St. Louis: Milliken Publishing Co., 1962, 1963) entitled *Read and Think* for the primer level through grade three and *Reading Adventures* for grades four and higher is an excellent source of material for fostering communication with greater accuracy. The series consists of books, two for each grade level, each containing about thirty individual duplicating master work sheets. Some of these are: Telling a Story in Order, Words with Two Meanings, Say It Right (this one requires the child to choose the best synonym to denote shades of verbal expression—for example, agreed John, grumbled John, gasped John; giggled Mary, whispered Mary, shouted Mary), and Words That Belong Together. A brief teacher's guide as well as answers are included in each book.

Myers, R. E., and Torrance, E. Paul. *For Those Who Wonder* (1966); *Can You Imagine* (1965); *Plots, Puzzles, and Plays* (1966). Boston: Ginn and Company. Each title in this series has a workbook and detailed, well-organized teacher's guide. Each workbook lists over twenty different activities, all of them geared toward fostering creativity, curiosity, a sense of humor, and imagination. Logical thinking is also highlighted, not as the antithesis of creativity, but in conjunction with it. Some of the exercises entail exploring one's feelings (for example, the pupil is asked his reaction to specific instances of advice such as "Always be polite to adults, especially to friends of your parents" and then to compare how he feels about getting advice with giving it), being less literal (for example, the pupil is asked to explain the apparent contradictions of such expressions as *silent cheering, triumphant loser, illiterate reader*), and developing empathy (the pupil is told to imagine that a few special objects can talk; he is then asked questions like "What would your pants or dress say to you when you spill ice cream on your lap?" "What would your bicycle or scooter say to you when you give it to someone else because you have a new bicycle or scooter?").

Although all the units in the workbooks entail considerable writing, this can easily be modified so that more oral expression is used.

The *Prentice-Hall Learning Systems* (Englewood Cliffs, N.J., 1977), entitled *Primary Pathways to Reading: Comprehension Skills,* consists of five books (numbered one to five), each containing twenty duplicating master work sheets. Each book covers four to five different skills and is arranged in order of difficulty. The books are geared to the primary reading grade levels. Some of the areas covered that are particularly pertinent toward the improvement of communication skills are: Interpreting Mood, Understanding Characters, Understanding Sequence, Forming Associations, Figures of Speech, Making Judgments, and Fact and Opinion.

GAMES

Body Language. Springfield, Mass.: Milton Bradley Co., 1975. This is a game of Charades. Players alternate between the roles of actor, guesser, and loader (the one who inserts the cards in the turntable). The actor attempts to dramatize the printed word he sees. He is allowed to use gestures and to make sounds but may not use any words or parts of words. Each message consists of individual words. Different parts of speech are used: nouns (e.g., bicycle, waiter, appendix, straw), verbs (e.g., swim, carry, wink, swallow), adjectives (e.g., straight, sour, stiff, warm), prepositions (e.g., up, in), expletive (e.g., ouch). The player receiving the signals must guess all of the messages (seven different cards are inserted in the turntable at each round) before the turntable stops spinning. This race against time adds to the novelty and excitement of the game. It is recommended for ages nine to adult.

The Talking, Feeling, and Doing Game. A Psychotherapeutic Game for Children, by Richard Gardner, M.D. Cresskill, N.J.: Creative Therapeutics, 1973. The purpose of this game is to enable the therapist to learn about the underlying psychological processes of children in a nonthreatening manner. Each player (the child and his therapist) places his piece at the start position, rolls the die, moves his piece, and, according to the color of the space on which it lands, selects a card from the appropriate pile. The green pile contains many *doing* cards: "Make believe you're sleeping." "Laugh hard and loud." "Make believe you're having a temper tantrum. [Tell] why are you so angry?" The other cards involve considerable feeling. Some of the yellow cards read, "What's something you could say that would make a person feel bad?" "How do you feel when you meet a new person?" The white cards contain messages like: "What's the most disgusting thing a person can do? Why?" "Say something that isn't very nice." "If you had to be changed into someone else, who would you choose to be? Why?" The players accumulate chips by responding to their cards' question or instruction as they proceed to the finish line. They are allowed not to respond to any item, if they so prefer.

The author of this game, a child psychiatrist, recommends it be used only by therapists. Hence it would have relevance to school psychologists and specially trained guidance counselors.

Teachers, in consultation with therapists, may revise the items so that they are oriented less to the psyche of the *individual* child, but instead emphasize nonverbal communication and talking about emotion, *in general*. This game is not recommended for parents.

Target Behavior, by Roger Kroth. Olatha, Kans.: Select-ED, Inc., 1972. This is, essentially, a diagnostic tool in game format. The playing board consists of twenty-five squares divided symmetrically into nine columns. Column one has one square and is entitled "Most Like Me," the next column, headed "Very Much Like Me," has two squares, "Like Me" has three, "A Little Like Me" has four, "Undecided" has five, "A Little Unlike Me" has four, "Unlike Me" has three, "Very Much Unlike Me" has two, and "Most Unlike Me" has one. There are two sets of twenty-five behavior cards—one relating to classroom behaviors (e.g., pokes or hits classmates, is quiet during class time, smiles frequently) and the other to home behavior (e.g., plays alone, has a messy room, gets ready for school on time). One set of cards is placed around the board, the teacher reads each to the child who then places it in the column that, in his opinion, best describes him. Since there are only twenty-five spaces (one for each card), the child is forced to be judicious in his placement. (He is allowed to move a previously placed card to make way for a new one.) When the board is filled, the results are recorded (scoring sheets are provided) and the game resumes, but this time the child is instructed to arrange the cards on the basis of *how you would like to be.* These results are also recorded, then compared with the original ones. Hence, the child's perception of his *real self* and his *ideal self* is revealed, enabling the teacher and child to select a particular "target behavior" for modification. Other uses include parents and the teacher sorting the child's behavior, then analyzing and discussing any differences in opinion. This game lends itself to such activities as the child discussing his feelings and emotions, and dramatization. A wide range of grades can be accommodated inasmuch as the teachers can design their own behavior cards appropriate for any level.

In addition to the playing board, the two sets of behavior cards, and the score sheets, the kit furnishes a well-organized and detailed instruction brochure.

Tell It Like It Is! The Ungame. Garden Grove, Calif.: Au-Vid Inc., 1972. Players move their markers across the board as many spaces as the roll of a die specifies. If they land on an orange space, they draw a card and "tell it like it is" in two or three sentences (Some of these cards ask: "What is your best friend like?" "What do you like to daydream about?" "What do you think your friends say about you when you're not around?"). If they land on a green space, they must "do their own thing" (make any comment on any subject, ask someone a question, or simply choose a "Tell It Like It Is" card); the board has words such as *loneliness, boredom, hope, anger, courage,* and *pride* scattered across it to suggest a mood or feeling the player might wish to share or ask someone about. If they land on a white space, they must read the statement aloud (each white space has a printed statement), respond accordingly, and explain their reasons if they wish. Some of the messages are: "If you were not patient today, go to the dumps." "If you have not laughed today, start over." "If you felt envy this week, go to left field." A set of yellow cards are provided for children of elementary school age, a set of white ones for adults and young adults, and a set of optional cards (orange) religiously oriented (Christian).

RECORDINGS

Meet Mr. Mix-Up, by Frank Gisonti. Freeport, N.Y.: Educational Activities, Inc. This material is available in cassette (AC 707) or LP Record (AR 707) form. Throughout a series of songs and rhymes, Mr. Mix-Up makes errors (absurdities, omissions, and so on), and the listener is encouraged to identify them and to offer corrections. This humorous approach helps children develop greater comprehension and listening skills; thus it nourishes communication with greater accuracy.

Mix-Up picture cards (a picture of a man in the rain holding an umbrella upside down, for example) are included as a warm-up to the record. These can be used independently in developing visual perception (that is, noting details and seeing the gist of a drawing).

My Moods and Feelings, by Lynn and Hy Glaser. Merrick, N.Y.: Ultrasound Record Company. The album consists of a separate song title for each of the following emotions: Happiness, Love, Anger, Fear, and Sadness (called "Unhappiness"). Additional moods and feelings are depicted in songs entitled: Shyness, Envy, Pretending, Giggling, and Feeling Good All Over. The lyrics and vocabulary render this record particularly suitable for the elementary school grades. A teacher's guide is included giving the lyrics for each song and including suggested questions and activities.

The same company publishes another record (written by the same authors) entitled *There's Nobody Like Me.* Self-awareness, self-concept, and self-esteem are heightened through such songs as "There's Nobody Like Me," "So What If I'm Not Perfect," "Give Me a Chance to Grow Up," "Isn't It Better Being You?" and "My Best Friend, Your Best Friend." Recommended for the elementary grades, this record is accompanied by a teacher's guide that lists suggested follow-up activities and discussion topics.

Who Said It? by Ernest Siegel, Frank Gisonti, and Gerald Posnack. Freeport, N.Y.: Educational Activities, Inc. This kit contains a cassette (AC 703) or an LP record (AR 703) and ten sets of picture-response cards. Four situations (teacher-pupil, doctor-patient, mother-daughter, and customer-salesman) are presented. Each situation contains a brief introduction that sets the scene, instructions to the students, and twenty direct quotations. The children must listen carefully and, after each comment, determine which of the two characters would most likely have said it. Since the same voice is used for all the direct quotations, and since each quotation is independent of the preceding one, decisions must be made on the basis of content alone. Hence this activity not only nurtures listening skills, but promotes empathy and logical thinking as well. Pupils can respond orally, in writing, or simply by raising the correct picture-response card.

INSTRUCTIONAL CARD SETS

Comprehension and Vocabulary Development Task Cards. Grand Rapids, Mich.: Instructional Fair, Inc., 1974. There is a separate kit for each of the grade levels, primary to grade eight. Each kit includes approximately sixty individual task cards. In general, the activities can be used to foster communication with accuracy, logic, and interest. Some of the topics included are: Fact and Opinion, Finding More Than One Meaning in Sentences, Ambiguity, Qualifying, Figurative Language, Analogies, Classifying, Ideas, Either-Or Statements, If-Then Statements, Contradictories, Exaggerations, Propaganda Recognition, Clichés, and Redundancy. A helpful "Definitions and Examples of Contents" card is included in each kit.

Got to Be Me, by Merrill Harmin. Niles, Ill.: Argus Communications, 1976. This kit includes forty-eight colored, humorously illustrated cards. Each card contains two unfinished sentences, one on each side. They are designed to make the child more aware of himself—his feelings, his hopes and dreams, his strengths and weaknesses, his likes and dislikes. Some examples are: "I laugh when————," "I am afraid to————," "I was really scared once when————," "I wish people would stop ————." Besides expressing his feelings orally, the child is able to write his thoughts since a workbook containing the same sentences, the identical pictures (but in black and white, hence permitting the child to color them), and writing space is provided. Finally, the kit contains a teacher's guide describing individual as well as group activities such as role playing and mock interviews.

171

Lifeline, by Peter McPhail. Niles, Ill.: Argus Communications, 1975. This is a Values Education program and is recommended for junior and senior high school pupils. The first stage, which can easily be used to promote role playing, drama, and pantomime, consists of three sets of colored, humorously illustrated activity cards. One set (comprised of forty-six cards) is called *Sensitivity Cards.* A situation is depicted and captioned (for example, "A boy in your class thinks it is amusing to let the air out of bicycle tires," "A friend of yours constantly talks about money and the cost of things"), followed by the words "What do you do?" Another set is made up of seventy-one *Consequence Cards.* A problem situation is portrayed and explained (for example, "Someone handles food without having washed his hands properly," "Someone is persuaded to start smoking cigarettes to be sociable"); the pupil is asked to consider "What could happen as a result of this action?" The final set is sixty-three *Points of View Cards,* each containing a drawing and the written script (or explanation). For example, one shows a middle-aged man berating an elderly lady for parking in his driveway. She says that she can't hear him, but he doesn't believe her. The student is asked such questions as "What do you think has gone wrong here, and why?" "How do you think the elderly lady felt in this situation?" "If you were the middle-aged man, how would you have approached this situation?" Besides serving as a springboard for activities that entail communication with expression and with emotions, these cards also promote productive decision making, logical thinking, empathy, and consideration of others.

The Outlining Kit (CAT. W174), by Herbert Hill and Joan McKenna. Woburn, Mass.: Curriculum Associates, Inc. This teaching aid is designed to help elementary and junior high school students learn how to compose and use outlines. It facilitates the development of logical thinking, ability to plan and organize, and creativity. Five broad categories—Finding Main Topics, Completing Outlines, Developing Ideas, Using Details, and Writing Paragraphs (using outlines that have been provided)—proceed sequentially from simpler to more complex tasks. The kit consists of 108

$6'' \times 9''$ lesson cards (designed so that students may work independently with minimum teacher direction), a teacher's guide, and nine spirit masters for pretests and posttests.

The same company publishes *Precise Word* and *Multi-Meaning* (CAT W238, by Robert Forest), which consists of one hundred cards and eighty cards respectively. Each *Precise Word* card presents three words that are similar in meaning with definitions that illustrate the shades of differences among them: e.g., cease—ending of some state or condition; discontinue—suspension of a habitual practice; stop—suspension of some motion, action, or progress. Three sentences appear under these, each requiring a single appropriate word choice; the author's suggested answers appear on the reverse side. Each *Multi-Meaning* card contains three definitions and the student must discover the single word that applies to all three definitions: e.g., Sometimes it is: (1) an apartment, (2) the footprint of a fox, (3) the floating leaf of the water lily. Answer (on the reverse side): pad.

Also published by this company are *Homonym Tales* (CAT W272, by Joyce Scinto) and *Word Tease, Idiomatry, Hidden Word II* (CAT W234, by Robert Forest). *Homonym Tales,* recommended for pupils in upper elementary and junior high grades, consists of thirty stories, each printed on a spirit master to facilitate duplication, and each containing a number of incorrect homonyms that are italicized and underlined. An answer card (the identical story using the correct spelling, also underlined and italicized) is provided. A chief purpose of this activity is to teach the pupil the proper meaning of commonly used homonyms. The *Idiomatry* kit consists of one hundred activity cards, each requiring the pupil to select the correct meaning of an idiom from three possible choices: e.g., When you *rub it in,* you: (a) massage the muscles, (b) repeatedly remind someone of his or her mistakes, (c) cause erasures. This training activity can be helpful in modifying an overly concrete thinking style, thereby enabling the pupil to communicate more logically and interestingly.

S.W.A.P., by Margaret Zeff and Doris Kitchens (Speaking with a Purpose—CTP 148). Monterey Park, Calif.: Creative

Teaching Press, Inc., 1976. The kit consists of a set of cards, each presenting a specific instructional activity. The cards are divided into four basic categories: Techniques (twenty-one cards), Practical Speaking (forty-one cards), Formal Speeches (thirty cards), and Listening (seventeen cards). Many of the activities emphasize speaking with feeling, with conviction, with precision, with logic (for instance, Excuses, Excuses, Practical #28, in which the pupil must think of an alibi *quickly* for going through a red light, breaking a neighbor's window with a baseball, etc.), with tact, with interest. Some of the activities involve individual performances, others entail group participation.

The same company publishes *Acting in Action,* by Joan Menuey and Anne Vener (CTP 149), 1975. Over one hundred creative dramatic activities—each on a separate card—foster skills in verbal as well as in nonverbal communication. They are divided into ten broad categories: The first is "Warm-ups" and its purpose is to help the players lose their inhibitions. Another section is "Changeovers," in which the player(s) portray—via pantomime as well as speech—specific moods (e.g., anger, excitement) or particular occupations (e.g., cook, thief, weight lifter). Additional ones include "Keeping the Story Going" (this promotes the ability to ad lib) and "The Part's the Thing" (entailing stage improvisation). The cards contain *Basic* as well as *Advanced* instructions, thus accommodating a large age range—from grades one through twelve.

PHOTOGRAPH SETS

The Many Faces of Childhood Posters (DLM #P225). Niles, Ill.: Developmental Learning Materials. The series is comprised of twelve large photographs; some are in color, others are black and white. Several depict individual children, the rest picture two or more people. The photographs express such emotions as happiness (some children clapping and laughing), tenderness (some children petting a duck), freedom (two boys running through a field), sadness (a child sitting on steps in a ghetto area), anger (a boy sitting in a chair, pouting), and loneliness (a boy walking by a brick wall). A thirteen-page teacher's guide is provided. For each of the photographs, procedural guidelines are presented and specific questions designed to stimulate classroom discussion are suggested.

The same company publishes a similar kit, *The Many Faces of Youth Posters* (DLM #P201). It also consists of twelve photographs. Some of the emotions expressed are contemplation (a boy with eyes almost closed and with his head resting on his hand), loneliness (a girl staring out of her window), joy (a girl walking down the street, smiling), and frustration and boredom (a girl leaning against a brick wall). One feature of the teacher's guide is that it includes comments written by teen-agers concerning their own ideas, feelings, and definitions of some of the depicted emotions.

Understanding Our Feelings, No. 1215. Paoli, Pa.: The Instructo Corporation. The kit embodies a set of twenty-eight black-and-white photographs of children and adults exhibiting a variety of facial expressions. Most of them are of individuals, a few depict two people. The photographs can be organized, for the sake of convenience, into two broad categories: pleasant emotions or unpleasant emotions. Of course, different individuals may interpret the mood portrayed by a given photograph in different ways. These photographs can be used to develop the idea that our feelings are often conveyed by facial expressions and to help children identify and label a variety of emotions. This kit can also help develop creativity (for example, the children can make up stories to go with the pictures), and in guidance lessons (for example, they can discuss their own feelings and how to cope with them).

In addition to the photographs, the publishers supply a brief teacher's guide that suggests many useful procedures.

FILMS, FILMSTRIPS, FILM LOOPS

Published by Learning Corporation of America, New York City:

The Merry-Go-Round Horse (silent film—eighteen minutes). A little French ragamuffin falls in love with a wooden merry-go-round horse. He watches dejectedly as it is sold to a wealthy child who later abuses it. The urchin and his friends "rescue" it. He grooms and cares for it. His love, magically, makes the horse come to life and they canter off into the forest.

Sometimes I Feel . . . (five color cartoon filmstrips with matching cassettes; running time ranges between three and twelve minutes). The stories, recommended for grades kindergarten through third, are simple and lend themselves to dramatization, pantomiming, discussion of feelings.

One strip, "Boy, Was I Mad!" depicts anger: A boy intends to run away, but is sidetracked instead by various engrossing adventures (riding with a junkman, watching a tall crane at work, studying ants). He returns home after a trying afternoon and is no longer angry. He tells his amused mother about all the interesting things he did.

Other strips in the set include "The Blah" (which deals with sadness), "Did You Ever?" (imagination), "Maxie" (loneliness), and "Giants Are Very Brave People" (fear).

Ready Set Read! (thirty-six Super 8 Film Loops, silent, running time: three to four minutes each). Although this set is designed as a Reading Readiness Program for children in grades kindergarten to third and for older children who have not yet mastered basic skills, many of the loops can be used effectively to promote social perception. For example:

"What Made Him Feel That Way?" Five brief episodes are shown. Each is a fragment of a story involving one or two characters whose feelings are acted out (but not verbalized). The audience, after studying the actors' facial expressions (and other body language signals) are instructed to identify the portrayed emotion and to compose a story explaining why the characters feel that way.

"What Would You Say?" Several brief incidents are shown in which a child interacts with another person (a clerk in a store, a policeman, an older person, a playmate). The audience observes the action, facial expressions, gestures, and so on, and supplies an appropriate dialogue.

"What's in the Box?" Two characters, a man and a lady, take turns revealing the content of a mystery box. (There is one box for the man, another for the lady.) They peek—or feel through—a hole in the box, and then pass on their clues through pantomime. Children must "read" the mime, assemble the clues, and guess what is in the box. Box one includes a goldfish, a skipping rope, a top, a balloon. Box two includes a rope, a pizza, a kitten, tools.

Published by Weston Woods, Weston, Conn.:

Mr. Koumal. This consists of five vignettes, each lasting about two minutes. This set, recommended for pupils of junior high school grade level, is animated. Some of the titles are "Mr. Koumal Carries the Torch," "Mr. Koumal Invents a Robot," and "Mr. Koumal Flies Like a Bird." The entire series is nonverbal; various emotions are illustrated by facial expression, gestures, posture, and the like.

Weston Woods also produces many motion-picture adaptations of children's books, which, though verbal, can stimulate class discussion of feelings and serve as a springboard into pantomiming and informed drama activities. Among these are:

Blueberries for Sal. A little girl and a baby bear find themselves with the wrong mothers as they pick blueberries on a Maine hillside. Iconographic, nine minutes, color.

Caps for Sale. A hat peddler decides to take a nap in the country. He awakens to find his caps have been snatched by a group of mischievous monkeys. Iconographic, five minutes, color.

Harold and the Purple Crayon. Harold draws his way in and out of adventures: He draws pies when he is hungry, mountains to climb for a better view, and a boat when the water rises. Animated, eight minutes, color.

PROGRAMS

Developing Understanding of Self and Others (DUSO D-2), by Don Dinkmeyer. Circle Pines, Minn.: American Guidance Service, Inc., 1973. The DUSO D-2 Program, although recommended by its publisher primarily for use with children in the seven- to ten-year age range, seems equally appropriate for socially immature and imperceptive children who are of junior high school age. The overall objective of DUSO D-2 is to give children a better understanding of social and emotional behavior. Throughout, the child is provided with a variety of experiences that stimulate emotional involvement and is encouraged in discovering relationships between his feelings, values, and behavior. The total program is comprised of eight interrelated major units:

Toward Self-Identity: Developing Self-Awareness and a Positive Self-Concept

Toward Friendship: Understanding Peers

Toward Responsible Interdependence: Understanding Growth from Self-Centeredness to Social Interest

Toward Self-Reliance: Understanding Personal Responsibility

Toward Resourcefulness and Purposefulness: Understanding Personal Motivation

Toward Competence: Understanding Accomplishment

Toward Emotional Stability: Understanding Stress

Toward Responsible Choice Making: Understanding Values

Each unit is further subdivided into subthemes, called cycles. (Unit I has five cycles, the others each have four.) Many of the cycles are particularly helpful in teaching children to receive and express nonverbal communication signals: for example, learning to express both positive and negative feelings (Unit II, Cycle B); learning to empathize with the feelings of others (Cycle C); learning what behavior is considered appropriate or acceptable in various groups (Unit III, Cycle B); learning what behavior is inappropriate or unacceptable in various groups (Cycle C).

All the cycles of activities are uniform. Each contain—in sequential order—a story, discussion of a poster, discussion of a problem situation, role-playing activity, puppet activity, discussion of a picture, a career-awareness activity, supplementary activities, and supplementary reading activities. Since each cycle provides more than enough activities for one week's presentation, some teachers may wish to use the program on a daily basis.

178

In the teacher's manual explicit instructions are given regarding each of the activities (discussion pictures, stories, puppets, role playing, and so forth). Anticipated problems—disruptive players, reluctant players, noise, restlessness—are discussed. Each cycle is described fully and explained in a systematic and unambiguous fashion.

Besides the manual, the kit contains:

Records or Cassettes. Seventeen 7" 33⅓ rpm records containing thirty-four stories (dramatized by children as well as by adults), a song for each unit (eight in all), and the introductory song, "That's Where It's At." (The thirty-four stories are printed in the appropriate cycles of the manual and may be read, either as an alternative to—or in conjunction with—the recordings.)

Posters. Thirty-three 15" x 19" colored posters. Each reviews the theme of one of the stories.

Role-Playing Activity Cards. Thirty-three 7" x 10" cards are designed to involve children in dramatizing situations indigenous to the particular theme of each cycle. Every card contains the purpose and precise instructions (to the teacher) for a different role-playing activity. The role-playing activities entail the *spontaneous* enactment of social situations, thereby facilitating the integration of thoughts, feelings, and behavior (including using nonverbal communication cues).

Puppet Activity Cards. These are similar to the Role-Playing Activity Cards except that they involve dramatization involving puppets.

Puppets. The eight puppets include two character puppets: Duso the Dolphin who is an empathic listener and helps children understand themselves and others, and Coho who is somewhat insensitive in the early activities, but who gradually becomes more accepting and understanding. The puppets are designed to be used in the Puppet Activities as well as in Career-Awareness Activities.

Discussion Pictures. Thirty-three 15" x 19" pictures are provided in order to stimulate spontaneous discussion of feel-

179

ings, attitudes, values, and purposes. (A Discussion Picture Instruction Card is included.)

Career-Awareness Activity Cards. Thirty-three 7″ x 10″ Career-Awareness Activity Cards tie in the DUSO themes with career awareness and exploration. Such settings as The Car Wash, The Ice-Cream Factory, The Grocery Store, The Lemonade Stand, and The Gas Station are included.

Discussion Guide Cards. Six 10″ x 12″ cards are included: (1) listen for feelings, (2) tell how you feel about things, (3) don't interrupt, (4) be with it, (5) talk with each other, and (6) be positive. These cards are introduced in the first activity of the DUSO D-2 in conjunction with a story entitled "Introducing Group Discussions."

Self- and Social-Development Activity Cards. Eight cards are provided that aim at helping children learn more about themselves and others. Some of the cards are related to one specific DUSO unit, others relate to several.

The same company publishes a DUSO D-1 Program (1970) also written by Don Dinkmeyer. It is recommended for use with children in the kindergarten and lower primary grades. The format, materials, and goals are similar to those of DUSO D-2. The eight units are entitled: *Understanding and Accepting Self; Understanding Feelings; Understanding Others; Understanding Independence; Understanding Goals and Purposeful Behavior; Understanding Mastery, Competence, and Resourcefulness; Understanding Emotional Maturity; Understanding Choices and Consequences.*

The MWM Program for Developing Language Abilities, by Esther H. Minskoff, Douglas E. Wiseman, and J. Gerald Minskoff. Ridgefield, N.J.: Educational Performance Associates, 1972. This program is appropriate for children in the five- to ten-year age range and focuses upon the remediation of the twelve specific areas of language assessed by the Illinois Test for Psycholinguistic Abilities (ITPA). Of the three overall processes—reception, association, and expression—comprising the ITPA as well as the MWM Program, it is the expression activities that are most pertinent to the remediation of nonverbal communication and social perception. The teacher's manual entitled *Expression: Verbal and*

Manual contains descriptions of manual expression activities such as: expressing feelings via facial expressions and body movements, using gestures (e.g., wag index finger back and forth—"that's bad"; hand cupped behind ear—"I can't hear you"), pantomiming with imagined object (e.g., winding and putting on a watch, putting paper in a typewriter and typing), play acting (e.g., a policeman stopping traffic, a supermarket checker), pantomiming of animal movements. The verbal expression portion includes activities such as labeling of facial expressions that portray different emotions, role playing, and dramatizations. Other activities in this phase of the program that can help develop more accurate and interesting conversationalists are: a questioning game similar to "Twenty Questions," story chaining (from three to eight children create a composite story orally, each "author" adding to the previous one's statement), and monologues—descriptive (e.g., a child describes how he ties his shoes) and imaginative (e.g., a child speaks about the TV program in which he'd like to participate, he relates what he'd do if he could perform magic).

The materials consist of a teacher's guide divided into three major sections: descriptions, directions, and resources; an inventory of language disabilities (a screening device to be used by the teacher in identifying children manifesting language learning disabilities); six different teaching manuals—each of which contains detailed instructions to the teacher including a description of each task, specific questions to ask, scripts; five workbooks; a record for teaching sound blending; pictures (150 picture cards of nouns, verbs, and descriptive words; fifteen stimulus scenes; twenty sorting cards; and six portraits); a word book containing four lists of words (nouns, verbs, descriptive words, and prepositions); a storybook consisting of thirty-seven different stories including questions about each; and the various teaching scripts that are part of the teaching manuals themselves.

Peabody Language Development Kits (PLDK), Level #3, by Lloyd M. Dunn and James O. Smith. Circle Pines, Minn.: American Guidance Service, Inc., 1967. This kit is recommended for children whose language ages range between seven and one half and nine and one half years and is designed primarily to stimulate receptive, associative (the so-called inner language—reasoning, seeing relationships), and expressive language. Twenty-three different types of activities comprise the program:

1. Activity Time (various group activities: e.g., games involving the handling of an object from child to child and stopping at a given sound)
2. Brainstorming Time
3. Classification Time
4. Conversation Time (conversations about various topics such as: occupations; what you like in a friend; interesting places you have visited; discussions of idiomatic expressions)
5. Describing Time (describing objects that have been examined visually, or tactually; describing the contents of a picture)
6. Dramatization Time
7. Following-Directions Time
8. Guessing Time (guessing pantomimed actions, specific locales suggested by the musical recording "Who Am I?" the answers in activities similar to the game "Twenty Questions," the answers to riddles, and so on)
9. Imagination Time (imagining oneself in various specific situations—for example, in a space capsule, imagining the beginning of a story when only the ending is given, imagining what a nonsensyllable word means when used in the context of a given sentence)
10. Information Time (general information including vocabulary as well as more definitive areas such as Roman numerals, concept of types of houses—for example, duplex, and geographic facts concerning specific states)
11. Listening Time
12. Looking Time
13. Memory Time
14. Patterning Time
15. Reasoning Time
16. Relationship Time
17. Rhyming Time

18. Sentence-Building Time (making sentences when presented with stimulus pictures, spoken phrases, or incomplete sentences)

19. Speech-Development Time (elaboration on simple sentences, such as "Here is a book," to make larger ones; identifying initial consonants; recognizing the meaning of sentences when spoken in unusual pause patterns)

20. Speed-Up Time (saying a long sentence in one breath, enunciating "tongue twisters," naming—within one minute —a list of objects belonging to a given category)

21. Story-Making Time

22. Touching Time

23. Vocabulary-Building Time

The teacher's manual contains 180 "Daily Lessons"—each covering three of the twenty-three activity areas—proceeding sequentially in order of complexity. Other materials include a set of 214 colored stimulus cards ($7'' \times 9''$) arranged in nine different categories; a set of twelve colored "I Wonder" cards ($18\frac{1}{2}'' \times 21\frac{1}{2}''$); a set of four records (depicting various musical instruments, places, or events, and sound sequences); a set of 500 plastic color chips for scorekeeping as well as for teaching color, sequencing, motor skills, and memory; and two hand puppets, especially helpful for motivating children.

These activities are extremely useful in enhancing social perception. Many of the Dramatization and Guessing activities involve pantomiming. Some of the Imagination activities entail interpretation of facial expressions, gestures, and tones of voice. Listening skills are nourished by the Listening, Following Directions, and Guessing activities. In addition, the overall format focuses upon social interaction and group participation, and, throughout, the teacher is encouraged to remain "low-keyed," allowing a maximum of *pupil* conversation.

Other PLDK kits include:

Level #1 (1965) for children with a mental age of four and one-half to six and one-half years.

Level #2 (1966) for children with a language range from six to eight years.

Level-P (1968, authored by Dunn, Smith, and Kathryn B. Horton) for children whose mental ages range between three and five years of age.

The kits vary somewhat from level to level. For example, PLDK #1 includes Critical-Thinking Time and Identification Time but omits Sentence-Building Time and Reasoning Time. PLDK #2 has a tape recorder as well as a "Teletalk" (the latter is a two-way intercommunication device designed for simulating such settings as an airplane/control tower communication system or a radio or TV microphone and receiver). PLDK Level-P is a much larger kit than the others. Among its materials are: a set of music cards containing words and music (color- and number-coded) for presentation by a xylophone (which is also provided); three puppets; a large cloth bag ("P. Mooney Bag") for activities that stress tactile identification and/or memory; two 22" tall mannequins; one disassembled mannequin for teaching the names and relative proportions of body parts; a set of twenty-one life-size plastic fruits and vegetables designed for activities including concepts of color, same-different, and size as well as for vocabulary building; a set of forty-five magnetic geometric shapes.

Social Learning Curriculum (SLC) by Herbert Goldstein. Columbus, Ohio: Charles E. Merrill Co., A Bell and Howell Co., 1974. This program is designed primarily to foster the social adjustment of special children—that is, those who have learning and/or behavioral impairments—and is geared to the primary grade level. The SLC is divided into ten curricular sections known as phases:

1. Perceiving Individuality
2. Recognizing the Environment
3. Recognizing Interdependence
4. Recognizing the Body (developing body usage)
5. Recognizing and Reacting to Emotions
6. Recognizing What the Senses Do
7. Communicating with Others
8. Getting Along with Others

9. Identifying Helpers (activities that teach the role of the various members of the school staff and the type of help they can render the students)
10. Maintaining Body Functions (gaining knowledge regarding the functions of the various body systems and basic strategies for maintaining health)

There is a separate book for each phase. Each book is divided into a series of lessons sequenced according to the principle of Gestalt psychology: That is, the first lesson presents the overall problem, subsequent lessons provide for differentiation and practice, and the last lesson integration. (To illustrate: In phase five, Recognizing and Reacting to Emotions, lesson one's objective is "The student should be able to recognize that there are situations that cause emotional reactions." Some of the subsequent lessons are entitled "Recognizing Happy Faces," "Recognizing Fear," "Recognizing Causes of Anger." The last lesson's objective is "The student should be able to identify specific emotions; causes of and changes in emotions; consequences of emotional reactions; degrees of emotions; and moods created by emotions.")

Every lesson lists the objective, preliminary "Teacher Information," materials, preparation, lesson strategies (the actual instructional activities), and additional strategies. The table of contents cites multiple objectives for each lesson. In addition, each phase book has an introduction section, and offers references for professional use and references for student use.

Besides the ten phase books, an overall teacher's guide is provided that states the basic philosophy and rationale for the SLC and explains its organization. Other materials comprising this kit are: ten spirit duplicating books, stimulus pictures, scope and sequence chart (listing the specific content areas of all ten phases), a book of suggested supplementary science activities, a physical education supplement, and a mathematics supplement.

Throughout the SLC, considerable social interaction is provided via the emphasis on group discussion, group games, and role playing.

Toward Affective Development by Henry Dupont, Ovitta Sue

Gardner, and David S. Brody. Circle Pines, Minn.: American Guidance Service, Inc., 1974. This program is designed to stimulate psychological and affective development and is recommended for use with students in grades three to six. It is comprised of five main sections that further divide into 21 units or 191 lessons. Each lesson includes one or more activities and is made to be used sequentially.

The activities in the first section, entitled "Reaching In and Reaching Out," promote group participation (listening to others, sharing ideas and feelings, etc.), stimulate curiosity, and provide students the opportunity to see themselves as others see them (for example, in one lesson, the class selects a Boy or Girl of the Week. The other students then tell all the things that the selected student does well). Other activities help students become more aware of what they see, hear, touch, taste, and smell, nurture creativity ("How many ways can you use a rubber band?" "Make a list of all the things you would like to take to the moon with you" etc.), and promote the verbalization of feelings and emotions.

Section two, "Your Feelings and Mine," endeavors to help students learn to recognize, label, accept—and gain insight into the underlying causes of—feelings, and to become aware that their own actions affect the emotional climate of the class. The activities are varied: one involves linking color to feeling (e.g., "blue mood," "in the pink"), another helps students relate simulated animal movements to feeling (e.g., "I feel big and strong," "I feel quick and sly"), still another is designed to illustrate the importance of timing in verbal communication. Others include drawing simplified facial expressions to match given sets of quotations, changing tones of voices to convey different emotions, and even the expanding of the students' affective vocabulary to include such words as *compassion, pride,* and *respect.*

Section three, "Working Together," helps students become more aware of specific feelings and actions that either weaken or strengthen group efforts. Understanding of their own feelings as well as empathy are heightened. The objective of section four, "Me: Today and Tomorrow," is to make students become more aware of their unique characteristics, aspirations, and interests. The last segment, section five, "Feeling, Thinking, and Doing," endeavors to help students develop constructive thought processes for resolving conflicts. The lessons include identifying alternate courses of actions, considering possible consequences, and choosing appropriate courses of action.

Other materials include a teacher's manual (309 pages), forty-four $10'' \times 14''$ illustrations (among which are silhouettes of posture and hand gestures, and pictures of facial expressions); ninety-three $15'' \times 19''$ colored discussion pictures designed to elicit discussions of the illustrated events and actions and of the probable feelings and actions of the characters (five of these are also in filmstrip form); a cassette consisting of four recordings designed to encourage listening skills, imagination, and awareness of feelings, and to provide creative writing experiences; two $25'' \times 38''$ posters; shapes and objects cards to be used in group membership activities and in increasing sensory awareness; two sets of thirty-seven illustrated career folders; duplicating masters for student activity sheets; plastic color chips to be used in lessons requiring pupil interaction and cooperation. Finally, the kit contains two unusual materials: (1) forty "Feeling Wheels" (each has words denoting common feelings printed in specific sections that are color-coded, e.g., red/angry) facilitate the identification and expression of feelings, and (2) a large, red scarf that often serves to identify the player whose turn it is to perform, functions as an "icebreaker," and promotes group discussion, interaction, and participation.

Bibliography

Bem, Daryl, and Bem, Sandra. "Case Study of a Non-Conscious Ideology: Training the Woman to Know Her Place." In Daryl Bem, *Beliefs, Attitudes and Human Affairs.* Belmont, Calif.: Wadsworth, 1970, pp. 89–99.

Birdwhistell, Ray. *Kinesics and Context.* Philadelphia: University of Pennsylvania Press, 1970.

Brammer, Lawrence M. *The Helping Relationship: Process and Skills.* Englewood Cliffs, N. J.: Prentice-Hall, 1973.

Bush, Wilma Jo, and Giles, Marion T. *Aids to Psycholinguistic Teaching.* 2nd ed., Columbus, Ohio: Charles E. Merrill Co., 1977.

Cedoline, Anthony J. *The Effect of Affect.* San Rafael, Calif.: Academic Therapy Publications, 1977.

Clark, Don. *Loving Someone Gay.* Millbrae, Calif.: Celestial Arts, 1977.

Connolly, Christopher. "Social and Emotional Factors in Learning Disabilities." In Helmer Myklebust, ed. *Progress in Learning Disabilities,* vol. 2. New York: Grune and Stratton, 1971, pp. 151–178.

Davitz, J. R. *The Communication of Emotional Meaning.* New York: McGraw-Hill, 1964.

Delaney, D. "Sensitization to Non-Verbal Communications." *Counselor Education and Supervision* 7 (1968): 315–316.

Dion, K., and Berscheid, E. "Physical Attractiveness and Sociometric Choice in Nursery School Children." Unpublished paper, 1971. Cited in E. Aronson, *The Social Animal*. San Francisco: W. H. Freeman and Co., 1972, p. 216.

Egan, Gerald. *The Skilled Helper: A Model for Systematic Helping and Interpersonal Relating*. Belmont, Calif.: Wadsworth, 1975.

Ekman, P., and Friesen, W. V. "The Repertoire of Non-Verbal Behavior: Categories, Origins, Usage, and Coding." *Semiotica* 1 (1969): 49–98.

Fantz, R. L. "Pattern Vision in Newborn Infants." *Science* 140 (1963): 296–297.

Flaste, Richard. "Life on the Sidelines: The Lonely Children." *The New York Times* (*Parents/Children syndicated column*) January 14, 1977, B4.

Furth, Hans G., and Wachs, Harry. *Thinking Goes to School: Piaget's Theory in Practice*. New York: Oxford University Press, 1975.

Giffin, Kim, and Patton, Bobby. *Fundamentals of Interpersonal Communication*. New York: Harper and Row, 1971.

Guilford, J. P. "An Experiment in Learning to Read Facial Expressions." *Journal of Abnormal Social Psychology* 24 (1929): 191–202.

Haggard, E. A., and Isaacs, K. S. "Micromomentary Facial Expressions as Indicators of Ego Mechanisms in Psychotherapy." In L. A. Gottschalk and A. H. Auerbach, eds. *Methods of Research in Psychotherapy*. New York: Appleton-Century-Crofts, 1966, pp. 154–165.

Hall, Edward T. *The Hidden Dimension*. Garden City, N.Y.: Doubleday and Co., 1966.

Harrison, R. P. *Beyond Words: An Introduction to Nonverbal Communication*. Englewood Cliffs, N. J.: Prentice-Hall, 1974.

Havighurst, Robert L. "Who Are the Socially Disadvantaged?" In Joe L. Frost and Glenn R. Hawkes, eds. *The Disadvantaged Child*. Boston: Houghton Mifflin, 1966, pp. 15–23.

Hebb, Donald O. *The Organization of Behavior*. New York: Wiley, 1949.

Hennings, Dorothy Grant. *Smiles, Nods, and Pauses*. New York: Citation Press, 1974.

Humphrey, George. "The Problem of Generalization." *Bulletin of Canadian Psychological Association* 4, no. 3 (October 1944): 37–51.

Johnson, Doris, and Myklebust, Helmer. *Learning Disabilities: Edu-*

cational Principles and Practices. New York: Grune and Stratton, 1967.

Keith, Robert L. *Speech and Language Rehabilitation: A Workbook for the Neurologically Impaired.* Danville, Ill.: The Interstate Printers and Publishers, Inc., 1972.

Kiesler, S., and Baral, R. "The Search for a Romantic Partner: The Effects of Self-Esteem and Physical Attractiveness on Romantic Behavior." nd. Cited in Ellen Berscheid and Elaine Walster, *Interpersonal Attraction.* Reading, Mass.: Addison-Wesley, 1969, pp. 113–114.

Knapp, Mark L. *Non-Verbal Communication in Human Interaction.* New York: Holt, Rinehart, and Winston, 1972.

Kronick, Doreen. "The Importance of a Sociological Perspective Towards Learning Disabilities." *Journal of Learning Disabilities* 9, no. 2 (February 1976): 115–119.

———. *What About Me? The Learning Disabled Adolescent.* San Rafael, Calif.: Academic Therapy Publications, 1975.

McCandless, Boyd. *Children: Behavior and Development.* 2nd ed. New York: Holt, Rinehart, and Winston, 1967.

Moshner, Frederic A., and Hornsby, Joan Rigney. "On Asking Questions." In Jerome S. Bruner *et al.,* eds. *Studies in Cognitive Growth.* New York: Wiley, 1966, pp. 86–102.

Moustakas, Clark E. *Loneliness.* Englewood Cliffs, N.J.: Prentice-Hall, 1961.

New York City Board of Education, Division of Educational Planning and Support, *Oral Communication: Grades K–6,* Curriculum Bulletin, 1976–1977, Series No. 2.

Piaget, Jean. *The Language and Thought of the Child.* London: Routledge and Kegan Paul, 1948.

Polak, Eddy. *Teacher's Aid.* Montreal: Quebec Association for Children with Learning Disabilities, 1976.

Reader's Digest, May 1977, p. 129.

Riddle, Evelyn, and Wall, Kathleen. *Reading Adventures, Grade 4–First Half.* St. Louis, Mo.: Milliken Publishing Co., 1963.

Rosenfeld, L. B. *Human Interaction in the Small Group Setting.* Columbus, Ohio: Charles E. Merrill, 1973.

Ross, Alan O. *Psychological Aspects of Learning Disabilities and Reading Disorders.* New York: McGraw-Hill, 1976.

———. "Tactual Perception of Form by the Brain-Injured." *Journal of Abnormal and Social Psychology* 49 (October 1954): 566–572.

Sarason, Seymour, *et al. Anxiety in Elementary School Children*. New York: Wiley, 1960.

Schachter, Stanley, and Singer, Jerome. "Cognitive, Social and Physiological Determinants of Emotional State." *Psychological Review* 69 (1962): 379–399.

Siegel, Ernest. *The Exceptional Child Grows Up*. New York: E. P. Dutton, 1974.

————. *Helping the Brain-Injured Child*. Albany, N.Y.: New York Association for the Learning Disabled, 1961.

Smith, Robert M. *Clinical Teaching*. 2nd ed. New York: McGraw-Hill, 1974.

Snyder, Mark. "The Self-Monitoring of Expressive Behavior." *Journal of Personality and Social Psychology* 30 (1974): 526–537.

Tagiuri, R. "Person Perception." In E. Aronson and G. Lindzey, eds. *The Handbook of Social Psychology*. 2nd ed. Reading, Mass.: Addison-Wesley, 1969, pp. 395–449.

Tannenbaum, P. "Initial Attitude Toward Source and Concept as Factors in Attitude Change Through Communication." *Public Opinion Quarterly* 20 (1956): 413–425.

Torrance, E. Paul. *Guiding Creative Talent*. Englewood Cliffs, N.J.: Prentice-Hall, 1962.

Trager, G. L. "Paralanguage: A First Approximation." *Studies in Linguistics* 13 (1958): 1–12.

Wacker, John. "The Dyslogic Syndrome." In *Texas Key*, state newsletter of the Association for Children with Learning Disabilities, September 1975.

Walster, Elaine, Aronson, V., Abrahams, D., and Rottmann, L. "Importance of Physical Attractiveness in Dating Behavior." *Journal of Personality and Social Psychology* 5 (1966): 508–516.

Wiig, Elisabeth H., and Semel, Eleanor Messing. *Language Disabilities in Children and Adults*. Columbus, Ohio: Charles E. Merrill, 1976.

Index